The ideals Christmas Treasury

Let us go back to the beauties
That are pocketed deep in our past--
The joys we relinquished with childhood
But which hauntingly linger and last!

Let us return to the Christmas
That remains with the children of time--
The Christmas of wonderful wishes,
Of stardust, and snowdrift, and chime!

Let us go back to the vision
Of evergreen peace in our rooms,
Gay ribbons on gifts of the giving,
And the Dream that consistently blooms.

Let us in piety wander
Where the veil of the centuries parts
To look at a Crib and an Infant,
And Christmas will live in our hearts!

Frank H. Keith

Editorial Director, James Kuse
Managing Editor, Ralph Luedtke
Photographic Editor, Gerald Koser

Contents

ISBN 0-517-332477
COPYRIGHT © MCMLXXVIII BY IDEALS PUBLISHING CORPORATION
MILWAUKEE, WIS. 53201
THIS EDITION IS PUBLISHED BY BONANZA BOOKS,
A DIVISION OF CROWN PUBLISHERS, INC.,
BY ARRANGEMENT WITH IDEALS PUBLISHING CORPORATION.
a b c d e f g h
BONANZA 1981 EDITION
MANUFACTURED IN THE UNITED STATES OF AMERICA

Contents

Holiday Preparations

A Little Town Whose Industry Was Christmas

SIXTY MILES NORTH of Nuremberg, Germany, high in the Thuringian mountains, deep in a forest of 80-foot-tall Christmas trees, sits the village of Lauscha. Its ornamentally decorated, slate-covered houses perch on steep streets nestled at the bottom of a narrow mountain valley. In the 1930s Lauscha looked like a storybook German town.

At that time most of the glass ornaments on American Christmas trees came from the immediate vicinity of this little town. Lauscha was the birthplace, in the 1840s, of a cottage industry that supplied virtually all blown-glass Christmas tree ornaments until just before World War I, when a Viennese company began to copy the Lauscha ornaments. Later, Polish and Czechoslovakian glassblowers did the same, but Lauscha remained the principal ornament maker for the United States up to World War II.

By 1930, approximately 2,000 homes and 6,000 people in the immediate vicinity of the hamlet were engaged in a craft almost unchanged since before the turn of the century. An ornament maker's home was his factory. His wife and family were its staff and assembly line. He had a small *Werkstatt*, or workshop, attached to his house.

If you dropped in on a glassblower unexpectedly, you would probably find him perched on a high stool, bent over his bench, clad only in his long underwear, a pair of brown leather slippers on his feet. Behind him, far from the flame of a gas burner, were drums of lacquer and a hot pot of silvering solution, a combination of silver nitrate, quicklime and milk sugar. Every glassblower had his own family formula.

His wife handled the tedious job of silvering the inside of the ornaments. She filled each one-quarter full with the solution, then shook it. To keep the silvering spreading evenly, she dipped the bulb in hot water several times. Uneven silvering showed through even after the ornament had been lacquered, and wholesalers would turn those ornaments down. After the coating was complete, she poured the excess solution into a basin where the silver was chemically separated to be used again. Then she hung the ornaments up to dry in rows from the ceiling rafters.

The following morning most of the silvered ornaments were dipped in various colored lacquers. The family grew so accustomed to the overpowering smell of lacquer that they scarcely noticed it, but others never got used to it. An importer who visited the village in the 1930s said that as you approached in a car, you could tell 100 feet away that you'd come to a glassblower's cottage.

All members of the family helped with the painted trimming that decorated many of the ornaments. When the paint was dry, the oldest child was entrusted with scoring the six-inch stems or "pikes" with a small blade coated with an abrasive. Once scored, the pike broke off easily and cleanly. Then the youngest child was given the job of fitting on little metal caps. Working 8 to 15 hours, a family could make from 300 to 600 ornaments a day, often six days a week.

Glassmaking began in Lauscha in the 1590s when religious persecution in the German province of Swabia forced groups of Protestant glassmakers to leave their homes. They were drawn to the Thuringian mountains by an abundance of wood, sand and limestone, the necessary ingredients for glassmaking. In 1597, with the help of the Duke of Coburg, they built a small glass factory in Lauscha.

Gradually, the village became a center for drinking glasses, bull's-eye window glass and other products which were sold by peddlers. But as more glassmakers were drawn to this center, authorities decided to limit new factories because of the heavy demand they were making on the wood supply from local forests. As a result, some glassblowers set up home workshops.

Now in East Germany, Lauscha nestles in the Thuringians. The old houses hark back to the days when every home was a small factory and most handmade products were aimed at Christmas.

Nowadays a few old-time glassblowers, like this one, carry on Lauscha's traditional cottage industry.

In the middle of the 18th century some of these craftsmen began to make glass beads, supplying jewelry and millinery trades throughout Europe. But glassblowers in Bohemia developed a method of making shinier beads than those produced in Lauscha, and almost overnight Lauscha lost most of its bead market. Hard times prevailed until a Lauscha glassmaker succeeded in duplicating the Bohemians' silvering formula. He saved the remnant of the town's business.

He also blew thick-walled glass balls which he silvered with his new mirroring solution. Since the 1820s heavy glass balls had been made by Lauscha craftsmen experimenting to see how large a bubble they could blow. They were known as *Kugeln* and many had been "silvered" inside with lead or zinc to make them reflect. Some were fastened to wooden crowns and hung from the ceiling during the Christmas season. The first written record of glass Christmas tree balls being produced was in 1848, when "six dozen of Christmas tree ornaments in three sizes" were recorded by a Lauscha glassblower.

In 1867 a gasworks was built in Lauscha. For the first time glassblowers had a steady, very hot, easily adjustable flame, making possible large, thin-walled bubbles of glass. A paper-thin, one-inch version of the old heavy *Kugel* was perfected. Glass ornaments were molded by blowing a bubble into a cookie mold. Soon glassblowers were producing pine cones, apples, pears and crystal icicles for tree ornaments. In a short time they were being exported to America.

American store buyers, including F. W. Woolworth, began making side trips to Lauscha while scouting for toys and dolls in nearby Nuremberg and Sonneberg. Ornament-making totally dominated the life of Lauscha and the neighboring village of Steinheid.

By 1890 the Lauscha glassblowers had perfected the use of molds. The top and bottom halves of a mold were glued to a set of iron tongs. By the 1930s this had evolved into a handmade iron device with a steel spring which was clamped upright on the workbench. It held the mold at the right height and allowed the glassblower to open and close it with a pedal.

Reheating the closed end of a thin tube of glass which he had just sealed over his gas burner, the craftsman blew a bubble the same shape and only a little smaller than the ornament he was about to make. Quickly, he placed the still orange-hot molten bubble in the bottom half of the mold and closed the top, leaving only the blowing end of the tube protruding through a small hole. Working

fast, before the glass could cool and alw blowing downward into the mold, he expan the thin glass bubble inside to fill the m After a few seconds, he opened the mold ar bird or acorn or some other recogniza shape emerged. The growing need for mc brought a new type of craftsmen to Lausch skilled artists or doll makers who could m anything the American importers asked i

Over the years, glassblowers of Laus reproduced every conceivable fruit and ve table—even including several differ pickles. Dogs, cats, monkeys and be abounded. Clowns and storybook charact were popular, as were the Christ Child, ang and the Christian symbol, the fish. A wh village of different little glass houses churches could be hung on the tree, objects like purses, pipes, drums, violins.

One of the most enduring patterns was bird with a spun-glass tail. Originally it hu from a delicate glass hook protruding from back or head. By 1900 glassblowers borrowed the clip from the clip-on car holder of the period, and the birds acqui either one or two metal spring legs, wh were soldered to the clip base before be glued into indentations in the bird's be

Many people remember or still have

…gile glass bird from grandmother's tree, but …v have ever seen the many different kinds …birds that were originally made. In addition …a number of small birds native to Germany, …dentifiable to most Americans, there were …katoos, parrots, owls and the now-extinct …senger pigeon. Regardless of species, most …ds, including a peacock, had a two-inch tail …de of hair-fine strands of spun glass. Those …ich didn't had a crinkly wire tail.

…Santa Claus figures were always fashioned …hout legs, rounding off at the bottom of …ta Claus' coat. Santas from Lauscha almost …ariably carried little Christmas trees. In the …30s Czechoslovakian glassblowers imitated …e German figures, but they never showed …ta Claus carrying a Christmas tree.

…Enthusiasm for balloon ascensions gripped …th Germany and the United States in the …90s and was reflected in balloon-shaped …naments, complete with wire-tinseled mesh …bes and embossed lithographic cutouts of …gels and Santa Claus riding in the gondola. …toring was similarly reflected on Christ- …as trees of the 1920s when Lauscha glass- …wers produced a tiny period car. And when …e teddy bear craze gripped America, many …ddies began appearing among the angels and …ta Clauses.

Some shapes were produced without molds. To make these, the glassblower pushed and pulled free-blown bubbles into different shapes while they were hot, using wooden tools and an asbestos-covered leather glove. They blew tiny teapots and annealed delicate spouts and handles to them. In the same manner they made trumpets, as well as lyres, anchors and butterfly bodies with spun-glass wings. The toadstool, considered a sign of good luck in Germany, was a common object

made without a mold. Trumpets that could be blown and bells that rang required the utmost craftsmanship, and one master craftsman blew, twisted and coaxed a thin rod of glass into a delicate eight-inch stork which stood majestically on a Christmas tree.

In Lauscha, Friday was the day for marketing ornaments. Wives would strap towering baskets of them on their backs, often with additional bundles tied alongside, and off they would go, looking like blackbirds waddling with half-spread wings, to catch the train for nearby Sonneberg where the warehouses were.

Sunday afternoons, when weather permitted, ornament makers fielded a soccer team against doll makers or truckers. After the game they returned to a beer hall and boasted exorbitantly about how many ornaments they had made that week, while consuming quantities of beer and bratwurst.

Traditionally, Monday was the day for the men to go to town to buy their supplies. But by the 1930s the system had begun to change. It was more efficient to have the collectors they worked for supply the glass rods and the five-gallon cans of lacquer, delivering these by truck. In some cases the collector's truck also began to call for the big baskets of ornaments. Woolworth, Kresge, Kress and America's largest independent importer, Max Eckardt, all had warehouses near Sonneberg; glassblowers now worked for one company.

The finished boxes of ornaments moved from Sonneberg by rail to the ports in the north of Germany. Steamship lines gave very good rates to America's ornament importers, for the lightweight Christmas tree balls made perfect "top cargo," filling the hold after it had almost reached its limit with heavy cargo.

The hard but somehow satisfying way of life of the glassblowers of Lauscha was totally disrupted in 1939. After the war the town found itself about ten miles inside East Germany. In 1949, in an effort to help the West German economy, the United States sent Max Eckardt and one of his sons to try to establish an ornament industry there. A number of Lauscha refugees lived in the Coburg area, only about 20 miles from their old homes, and there was still a market for the fragile, hand-blown and decorated ornaments.

So between 1950 and the early 1960s about 20 percent of America's ornaments were again imported from Germany. A school for glassblowers was started in Neustadt, West Germany, only a mile from the border, and the old Lauscha men trained up to 15 young glassblowers a year. But the work was hot and hard, and as the West German economy boomed, there was too much "quick money" to be made elsewhere, with medical insurance and pensions thrown in. If an ornament maker's son wanted to follow his father's trade, his sweetheart would remind him, "Hans already owns a Volkswagen and you have only a motor scooter." Few young girls in the new Germany dreamed of working as hard as the cottage workers' wives had.

About 600 glassblowers and their families moved to West Germany by sneaking through the woods on dark nights. Among those who stayed in Lauscha, a ten-year-long black market in Christmas tree ornaments developed. On foggy nights Lauscha men stealthily carried bundles of their fragile glass ornaments, rolled in tablecloths, to silent border meetings where they were slipped under the barbed wire. In return they got razor blades, coffee, cigarettes and other commodities hard to obtain in the Eastern Zone.

By the 1960s, times had improved on both sides of the border but, East or West, the ornament makers continued to have little except the satisfaction of their work. Today, in West Germany, fewer people make ornaments by hand with every passing year. And in Lauscha only a few old men, too old to work regularly, still blow ornaments in their homes. Others blow them on a production line at the town's government factory. They may even use a number of their old molds. But few of these fragile, fanciful ornaments now find their way to America, where the Christmas tree is ever more likely to be decked with plastic.

Phillip Snyder

The most prestigious residence in America is the White House, and no holiday calls for more lavish decorations than Christmas. So it is no surprise that we look to the White House at Christmas to learn about some of the most exciting and elegant celebrations in the history of our country.

Because Christmas is an especially thrilling holiday for children, many of our presidents have chosen this time to entertain youngsters. Thomas Jefferson, the first president to live in the White House, gave a party for his grandchildren and one hundred guests. The president himself, as master of ceremonies, had his pet bird do tricks and later he played the violin so the young guests could dance.

Andrew Jackson, perhaps the least formal White House resident, gave a children's party that included a game of hide-and-seek in the East Room. After snacks in the State Dining Room, the guests returned to the East Room for a snowball fight—with artificial snowballs, made of cotton and each containing a piece of candy.

Twentieth-century presidents also loved to entertain young people at Christmastime. Theodore Roosevelt's wife, Edith, gave a "no adults allowed" party one year. If any of the six hundred guests were accompanied by nurses or parents, the grown-ups had to stay downstairs during the party.

No president gave more children's parties than Lyndon Johnson—each year he and his daughters hosted a series of them. One year Luci Johnson gave a party for needy children at which a staff member dressed as Santa Claus presented them all with gifts.

Christmas is also a time for family traditions, and several presidents either brought their holiday rituals to the White House or created new ones while they were there. Rutherford Hayes, on his first Christmas in the Executive Mansion, had a dollhouse built for his daughter. It has

since become a Hayes family heirloom. Calvin Coolidge loved to listen to his church choir singing carols at Christmastime. When he was president, he invited the entire choir to the White House to sing. And Franklin Roosevelt read Charles Dickens' *A Christmas Carol* to his children every year, even after they were grown up and had families of their own.

Decorations have always been a cherished part of American Christmases. They have played an important part in White House holidays as well. The favorite modern American holiday decoration, the Christmas tree, was introduced to the White House in 1889 by Benjamin Harrison, who put a decorated tree in the oval room on the second floor. Grover Cleveland, whose second term in office followed Harrison's term, had a Christmas tree downstairs for a carnival he gave for his children and those of cabinet members.

The Christmas tree custom mushroomed through the years. When Dwight Eisenhower was in office, he had dozens of trees, including a huge, formally decorated one in the East Room. The Nixons had one large cut tree in the Blue Room and a family tree upstairs. In various parts of the house they placed potted trees, which were later planted in parks. The Gerald Ford family enjoys using traditional handcrafted Christmas tree ornaments. In 1975, the large tree in the Blue Room was decorated with three thousand handmade ornaments, from cookies to crocheted snowflakes to corn dollies.

These are only a few of the ways that United States presidents have celebrated Christmas. All of the presidents had distinctive styles, some of them quite formal and others surprisingly casual. We can be sure that as new families move into the Executive Mansion they too will use their own imaginations, so that we will continue to find innovative and exciting celebrations at Christmas at the White House.

Michael Phillip Manheim

Christmas

at the White House

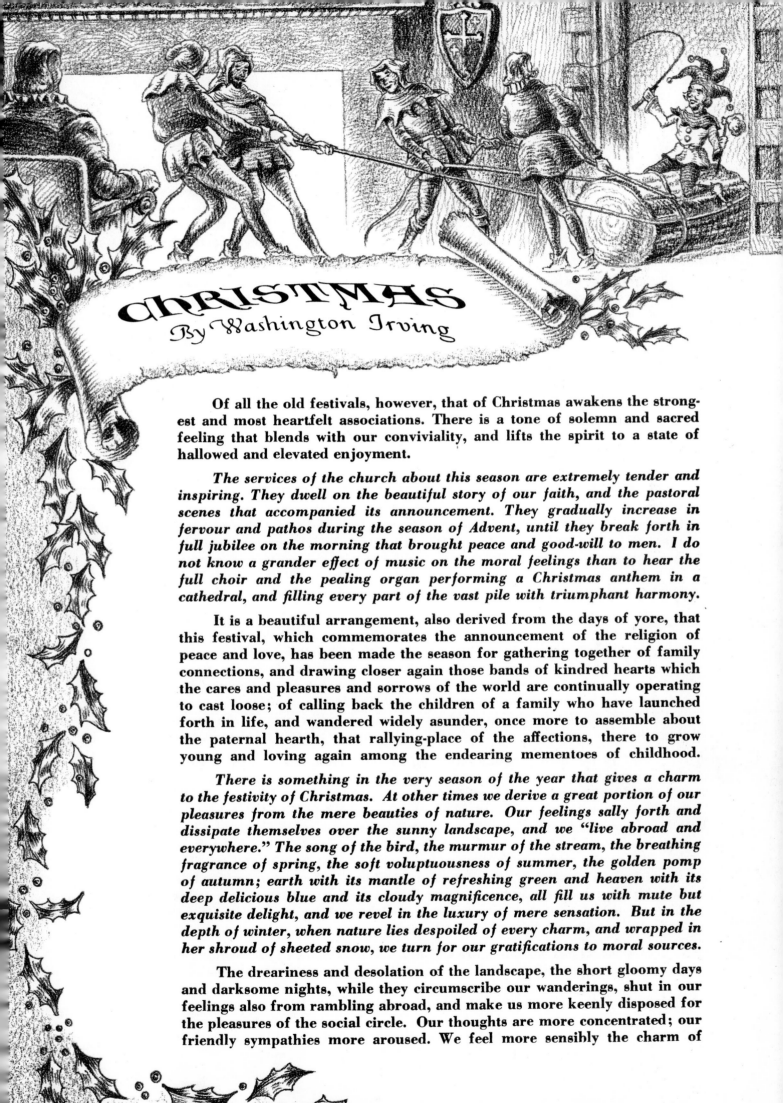

CHRISTMAS
By Washington Irving

Of all the old festivals, however, that of Christmas awakens the strongest and most heartfelt associations. There is a tone of solemn and sacred feeling that blends with our conviviality, and lifts the spirit to a state of hallowed and elevated enjoyment.

The services of the church about this season are extremely tender and inspiring. They dwell on the beautiful story of our faith, and the pastoral scenes that accompanied its announcement. They gradually increase in fervour and pathos during the season of Advent, until they break forth in full jubilee on the morning that brought peace and good-will to men. I do not know a grander effect of music on the moral feelings than to hear the full choir and the pealing organ performing a Christmas anthem in a cathedral, and filling every part of the vast pile with triumphant harmony.

It is a beautiful arrangement, also derived from the days of yore, that this festival, which commemorates the announcement of the religion of peace and love, has been made the season for gathering together of family connections, and drawing closer again those bands of kindred hearts which the cares and pleasures and sorrows of the world are continually operating to cast loose; of calling back the children of a family who have launched forth in life, and wandered widely asunder, once more to assemble about the paternal hearth, that rallying-place of the affections, there to grow young and loving again among the endearing mementoes of childhood.

There is something in the very season of the year that gives a charm to the festivity of Christmas. At other times we derive a great portion of our pleasures from the mere beauties of nature. Our feelings sally forth and dissipate themselves over the sunny landscape, and we "live abroad and everywhere." The song of the bird, the murmur of the stream, the breathing fragrance of spring, the soft voluptuousness of summer, the golden pomp of autumn; earth with its mantle of refreshing green and heaven with its deep delicious blue and its cloudy magnificence, all fill us with mute but exquisite delight, and we revel in the luxury of mere sensation. But in the depth of winter, when nature lies despoiled of every charm, and wrapped in her shroud of sheeted snow, we turn for our gratifications to moral sources.

The dreariness and desolation of the landscape, the short gloomy days and darksome nights, while they circumscribe our wanderings, shut in our feelings also from rambling abroad, and make us more keenly disposed for the pleasures of the social circle. Our thoughts are more concentrated; our friendly sympathies more aroused. We feel more sensibly the charm of each other's society, and are brought more closely together by dependence on each other for enjoyment. Heart calleth unto heart; and we draw our pleasures from the deep wells of living kindness, which lie in the quiet recesses of our bosoms: and which when resorted to, furnish forth the pure element of domestic felicity.

The pitchy gloom without makes the heart dilate on entering the room filled with the glow and warmth of the evening fire. The ruddy blaze diffuses an artificial summer and sunshine through the room, and lights up each countenance into a kindlier welcome. Where does the honest face of hospitality expand into a broader and more cordial smile — where is the shy glance of love more sweetly eloquent — than by the winter fireside? And as the hollow blast of wintry wind rushes through the hall, claps the distant door, whistles about the casement, and rumbles down the chimney, what can be more grateful than that feeling of sober and sheltered security with which we look around upon the comfortable chamber and the scene of domestic hilarity?

The English, from the great prevalence of rural habits throughout every class of society, have always been fond of those festivals and holidays which agreeably interrupt the stillness of country life; and they were, in former days, particularly observant of the religious and social rites of Christmas. It is inspiring to read even the dry details which some antiquarians have given of the quaint humours, the burlesque pageants, the complete abandonment to mirth and good-fellowship, with which this festival was celebrated. It seemed to throw open every door, and unlock every heart.

It brought the peasant and the peer together, and blended all ranks in one warm generous flow of joy and kindness. The old halls of castles and manor-houses resounded with the harp and the Christmas carol, and their ample boards groaned under the weight of hospitality. Even the poorest cottage welcomed the festive season with green decorations of bay and holly — the cheerful fire glanced its rays through the lattice, inviting the passenger to raise the latch, and join the gossip knot huddled around the hearth, beguiling the long evening with legendary jokes and oft-told Christmas tales.

One of the least pleasing effects of modern refinement is the havoc it has made among the hearty old holiday customs. It has completely taken off the sharp touchings and spirited reliefs of these embellishments of life, and has worn down society into a more smooth and polished, but certainly a less characteristic surface. Many of the games and ceremonials of Christmas have entirely disappeared, and like the sherris sack of old Falstaff, are become matters of speculation and dispute among commentators. They flourished in times full of spirit and lustihood, when men enjoyed life roughly, but heartily and vigorously; times wild and picturesque, which have furnished poetry with its richest materials, and the drama with its most attractive variety of characters and manners.

The world has become more worldly. There is more of dissipation, and less of enjoyment. Pleasure has expanded into a broader, but a shallower stream, and has forsaken many of those deep and quiet channels where it flowed sweetly through the calm bosom of domestic life. Society has acquired a more enlightened and elegant tone; but it has lost many of its strong peculiarities, its homebred feelings, its honest fireside delights. The

traditionary customs of golden-hearted antiquity, its feudal hospitalities, and lordly wassailings, have passed away with the baronial castles and stately manor-houses in which they were celebrated. They comported with the shadowy hall, the great oaken gallery, and the tapestried parlour, but are unfitted to the light showy salons and gay drawing-rooms of the modern villa.

Shorn, however, as it is, of its ancient and festive honours, Christmas is still a period of delightful excitement in England. It is gratifying to see that home feeling completely aroused which seems to hold so powerful a place in every English bosom. The preparations making on every side for the social board that is again to unite friends and kindred; the presents of good cheer passing and repassing, those tokens of regard, and quickeners of kind feelings; the evergreens distributed about the houses and churches, emblems of peace and gladness; all these have the most pleasing effect in producing fond associations, and kindling benevolent sympathies.

Even the sound of the waits, rude as may be their minstrelsy, breaks on the mid-watches of a winter night with the effect of perfect harmony. As I have been awakened by them in that still and solemn hour, "when deep sleep falleth upon man," I have listened with a hushed delight, and connecting them with the sacred and joyous occasion, have almost fancied them in another celestial choir, announcing peace and good-will to mankind.

How delightfully the imagination, when wrought upon by these moral influences, turns everything to melody and beauty: The very crowing of the cock, who is sometimes heard in the profound repose of the country, "telling the night-watches to his feathery dames," was thought by the common people to announce the approach of this sacred festival.

Amidst the general call of happiness, the bustle of spirits, and stir of the affections, which prevail at this period, what bosom can remain insensible? It is, indeed, the season of regenerated feeling — the season for kindling, not merely the fire of hospitality in the hall, but the genial flame of charity in the heart.

The scene of early love again rises green to memory beyond the sterile waste of years; and the idea of home, fraught with fragrance of home-dwelling joys, reanimates the drooping spirit, — as the Arabian breeze will sometimes waft the freshness of the distant fields to the weary pilgrim of the desert.

Stranger and sojourner as I am in the land — though for me no social hearth may blaze, no hospitable roof throw open its doors, nor the warm grasp of friendship welcome me at the threshold,—yet I feel the influence of the season beaming into my soul from the happy looks of those around me.

Surely happiness is reflective, like the light of heaven; and every countenance, bright with smiles, and glowing with innocent enjoyment, is a mirror transmitting to others the rays of a supreme and ever shining benevolence. He who can turn churlishly away from contemplating the felicity of his fellow beings, and sit down darkling and repining in his loneliness when all around is joyful, may have his moments of strong excitement and selfish gratification, but he wants the genial and social sympathies which constitute the charm of a merry Christmas.

Winter Wonderland

Winter Landscape

Richie T. Weikel

High above the tree tops
My window frames a scene —
A lovely winter mural
So peaceful and serene;
The starlit skies
Shed a mystic light
O'er the snowclad world
On this Christmas night.

And the snowflakes fall
O'er the pale moon's face,
A dainty white veil
Of starspun lace.
The trees like specters,
Garbed in white,
Stretch silvery arms
In the pale moonlight.

And majestic pines
Sway to and fro,
As a brisk wind banks
The drifting snow.
May the words of our Lord
Spread good will o'er the earth,
Bring peace to all peoples
On this day of His birth.

The snowflakes ice the barnyard fences;
Inside, the embered hearth is warm;
The holly gathered from the woodlands
Is berry-red throughout the home.
The kitchen smells of ham, and sausage,
And bread that's baked with loving care;
The cedar bowed with satin ribbons
Holds popcorn balls and angel hair.

Christmas in the Country

The stars look down with quiet splendor
On candles gleaming through the pines;
The moon seems near in heaven's luster,
And how sublime its fullness shines!
Tonight the rural people mingle,
Unite their joys in glad refrain,
As carols ring beyond the chapel
With wondrous hope and peace again!

Inez Franck

Wishes from the Mountains

Merry Christmas from the mountains,
From the scented pines in white;
From the flame and lemon sunset,
From the yule logs' crackled light.
Merry Christmas from the rivers
Bubbling free and swift and clear;
Merry Christmas from the meadows
Streaked with silent running deer.

Christmas Eve is hushed and holy
With its message time-undimmed;
From the vast and candled skies come
Christmas wishes on the wind:

May the mountains' own Great Spirit
Make your life a singing stream;
May the twelve new moons now coming
Bring a purpose to your dreams.
May a rainbow touch your shoulder
With a promise in its glow;
May your moccasins leave hints of
Happy tracks in many snows.

Virginia Covey Boswell

A LOOK BACK AT

POCAHONTAS. LANCET PRINCE GREY EDDY GENERAL DARCY FLORA TEMPLE. LANTERN LADY WOODRUFF BROWN DICK ALICE GREY

ENTERED ACCORDING TO ACT OF CONGRESS IN THE YEAR 1856 AT CURRIER & IVES IN THE CLERKS OFFICE OF THE DISTRICT COURT OF THE SOUTHERN DISTRICT OF NEW YORK

REPRINTED FROM LITH. BY CUR

"TROTTING CRACKS" ON THE SNOW.

AMERICA'S SLED AND SLEIGH DAYS

Mary Carolyn McKee

Of the hundreds of Currier & Ives prints portraying American life a century or so ago, the most popular of all were, and are, the winter scenes. These snowscapes, although somewhat sentimentalized, presented an authentic record of winter living, and many of them featured the vehicles that were then the common means of transport for nearly everyone: sleds and sleighs. Back when the ''gasoline buggy'' was far in the future and the snowmobile not even a dream, many people looked forward to hitching up these carriers for local travel over the snow.

Winter travel on runners was much faster and easier in many parts of the country than travel on wheels in the summer when roads were deeply rutted and, when rains were heavy, turned into rivers of mud. On farms, large sleds were used to haul blocks of ice from ponds, logs from the woods, and feed for the stock. With their floors covered with straw or blankets, the sleds carried families to market, to church services, and on neighborhood visits. Lighter and often quite elegant sleighs were used for party-going or simply for the fun of racing along snow-covered roads.

According to early accounts, the forerunner of these

T H E R O A D , — W I N T E R .

versatile winter vehicles was a crude ground sled or ''drag'' invented by the American Indians. It consisted of two poles connected with another pole or a platform of sticks. Sometimes a hide basket was lashed to these crosspieces. On these simple sleds the Indians hauled firewood, animals killed in the hunt, and even tents. Since they were usually quite narrow, they could be pulled along the forest trails by hand using thongs, or the thongs could be hitched to a dog or horse.

Early American farm sleds were almost as primitive. Two pieces of wood were shaped into runners and fastened together with slats. Later, wooden or metal runners were attached to box-like wagon beds.

The first sleighs, like most of the carriages and coaches in colonial days, were heavy and cumbersome until an enterprising young man from Connecticut revolutionized sleigh styles in the early nineteenth century. James Brewster, a descendant of Elder Brewster of *Mayflower* fame, was apprenticed to a Massachusetts carriage builder for a number of years. In 1809 he had set out for New York City by stagecoach to seek another position. When the coach broke down in New Haven, Connecticut, and the passengers had to wait for repairs, Brewster walked about town and chanced to meet the owner of the town's first carriage company. When the builder offered him a job, he accepted it and forgot about New York.

Within a year he had launched his own carriage and sleigh business in New Haven. Brewster sleighs were marvels of grace and style as they skimmed lightly over the snow. There were models with one and two seats. More elaborate sleighs provided a seat for the coachman, and there were small ''pony sleighs'' to delight children. There were even ''push sleighs'' to be occupied by warmly dressed ladies and propelled from behind over the ice of ponds and lakes by their escorts on skates.

Sleighs and sleigh bells were natural companions, for sleigh bells were to sleighs as horns are to automobiles. On winter evenings they prevented collisions, warned pedestrians, and filled the winter air with their cheerful sounds. Sleigh bells became big business in East Hampton, Connecticut, where William Barton started making them about 1808. At one time there were at least thirty bell companies in town and East Hampton became popularly known as ''Jingletown.'' The bells came in a variety of sizes and patterns and were either single- or double-throated. The single-throated type had one slit to let out the sound; the double-throated variety had two slits cutting across each other at right angles. There were some twenty sizes of common sleigh bells, ranging from

seven-eighths of an inch in diameter to more than thre inches. They were strung together and sold by th pound, or riveted to the neck- or body-straps of horse. Bells with the sweetest tone were cast fror ''bell metal,'' a combination of tin and copper. Othe less expensive versions were simply stamped out o steel or brass.

There was always something wonderfully exhilarat ing about the ring of sleigh bells across a winter land scape. Edgar Allan Poe expressed this in the firs stanza of *The Bells:*

> *Here the sledges with the bells—*
> *Silver bells!*
> *What a world of merriment their*
> *melody foretells!*
> *How they tinkle, tinkle, tinkle*
> *In the icy air of night*
> *While the stars that oversprinkle*
> *All the heavens, seem to twinkle*
> *With a crystalline delight . . . .*

Some years after Poe's poem appeared, J. S. Pier pont, a minister from Litchfield, Connecticut, pai tribute to the joys of sleighing. He wrote for a Sunda School entertainment one of the most popular winte songs ever written. His *Jingle Bells* catches the hig spirits of sleigh riders who glide over the snow on winter evening:

> *Dashing through the snow*
> *In a one-horse open sleigh,*
> *O'er the fields we go*
> *Laughing all the way;*
> *Bells on bobtail ring,*
> *Making spirits bright;*
> *What fun it is to ride and sing*
> *A sleighing song tonight.*

That the jingle of the bells was reassuring after storm is pointed out in John Greenleaf Whittier' *Snowbound.* In the morning following the great snow fall, all was silent until the shut-ins ''heard once more the sleigh bells' sound,'' and knew that soon lif would be back to normal.

Sleighing was all the rage in America from abou 1830 to almost the end of the century, and it gave th streets of cities such as New York and Boston the loo of a gala winter festival. Stable owners welcome weather that would bring a rush of business—horse were groomed, sleighs made ready, and harnes polished when the air ''smelled like snow.''

Daring young drivers often raced their sleighs i areas of suburban Boston. Occasionally there wer smash-ups due to the heady combinations of fas

Entered according to act of Congress in the Year 1859 by Currier & Ives, in the Clerk's Office of the Dist! Court of the Southern Dist! of N.Y. *REPRINTED FROM LITH. BY CURRIER & IVES.*

THE SLEIGH RACE.

orses and speedy sleighs, but the popular sport rived. Two huge sleighs, ''Cleopatra's Barge'' and e ''Mammoth Mayflower,'' cruised the streets of the assachusetts capital after a big snowfall. Both re-mbled ships mounted upon runners and were drawn y several teams of strong horses. They often carried argoes of more than twenty passengers around the ty or out into the country.

It should be noted that not quite everyone consid-ed sleighing a delightful pastime. Harriet Mar-neau, a British writer who visited America in the late 830s and wrote *Retrospect of Western Travel* was a ssenter. She described the sport: ''Set your chair on springboard out on the porch; put your feet in a pail ll of powdered ice; have somebody jingle a bell one ear and somebody blow into the other ith a bellows, and you will have an exact idea of eighing.''

However, Charles Dickens, who visited America in 867 (his second journey), had an entirely different action. He chanced to be in New York City during a owstorm that was severe enough to stop train service or a time. In a letter to one of his daughters, Dickens described the city streets as bordered with high walls of sparkling ice and, ever delighted with a dramatic situation, wrote, ''I turned out in a rather gorgeous sleigh yesterday with any quantity of buffalo robes and made an imposing appearance.''

The use of sleds and sleighs continued through the 1890s but slowly waned after the turn of the century. As late as 1902 the Sears & Roebuck catalog featured a ''cutter'' department with illustrations of two one-horse vehicles priced at $16.90 and $22.50. A two-seated ''Russian'' bob sleigh was offered for $46.90.

Today one occasionally sees horse-drawn sleighs gliding along the side roads in New England, the Pennsylvania Dutch country, and the Middle West. The delight of antiques collectors, they add a nostalgic Currier & Ives touch to the snowscape.

One of this writer's earliest winter recollections was watching a cutter dash down a Missouri lane. With bells a-jingle, it drew up with a burst of speed before our gate. My uncle and aunt and their two small boys threw aside the fur robe and stepped out.

What a thrilling arrival that was! And what an excit-ing memory!

This article is reprinted from the December 1974 issue of EARLY AMERICAN LIFE Magazine with the permission of the publisher.

The Warmth of Home at Christmas

God Bless Us Every One

from

A Christmas Carol

by

Charles Dickens

Then up rose Mrs. Cratchit, Cratchit's wife, dressed out but poorly in a twice-turned gown, but brave in ribbons, which are cheap, and make a goodly show for six pence; and she laid the cloth, assisted by Belinda Cratchit, second of her daughters, also brave in ribbons; while Master Peter Cratchit plunged a fork into the saucepan of potatoes, and getting the corners of his monstrous shirtcollar (Bob's private property, conferred upon his son and heir in honor of the day) into his mouth, rejoiced to find himself so gallantly attired, and yearned to show his linen in the fashionable Parks.

And now two smaller Cratchits, boy and girl, came tearing in screaming that outside the baker's they had smelled the goose, and known it for their own; and basking in luxurious thoughts of sage and onion, these young Cratchits danced about the table, and exalted Master Peter Cratchit to the skies, while he (not proud, although his collars nearly choked him) blew the fire, until the slow potatoes, bubbling up, knocked loudly at the saucepanlid to be let out and peeled.

"What has ever got your precious father, then?" said Mrs. Cratchit. "And your brother, Tiny Tim? And Martha warn't as late last Christmas Day by half an hour!"

"Here's Martha, mother," said a girl, appearing as she spoke.

"Here's Martha, mother!" cried the two young Cratchits.

"Hurrah! There's such a goose, Martha!"

"Why, bless your heart alive, my dear, how late you are!" said Mrs. Cratchit, kissing her a dozen times, and taking off her shawl and bonnet for her with officious zeal.

"We'd a deal of work to finish up last night," replied the girl, "and had to clear away this morning, mother!"

"Well! Never mind so long as you are come," said Mrs. Cratchit. "S'it ye down before the fire, my dear, and have a warm, Lord bless ye!"

"No, no! There's father coming," cried the two young Cratchits, who were everywhere at once. "Hide, Martha, hide!"

So Martha hid herself, and in came little Bob, the father, with at least three feet of comforter, exclusive of the fringe, hanging down before him, and his threadbare clothes darned up and brushed to look seasonable, and Tiny Tim upon his shoulders. Alas for Tiny Tim, he bore a little crutch, and had his limbs supported by an iron frame!

"Why, where's our Martha?" cried Bob Cratchit, looking around.

"Not coming," said Mrs. Cratchit.

"Not coming!" said Bob, with a sudden declension in his high spirits; for he had been Tim's blood-horse all the way from church and had come home rampant. "Not coming upon Christmas Day!"

Martha didn't like to see him disappointed, if it were only in joke; so she came out prematurely from behind the closet door, and ran into his arms, while the two young Cratchits hustled Tiny Tim, and bore him off into the washhouse, that he might hear the pudding singing in the copper.

"And how did little Tim behave?" asked Mrs. Cratchit, when she had rallied Bob on his credulity, and Bob had hugged his daughter to his heart's content.

"As good as gold," said Bob, "and better. Somehow he gets thoughtful, sitting by himself so much, and thinks the strangest things you ever heard. He told me, coming home, that he hoped the people saw him in the church, because he was a cripple, and it might be pleasant to them to remember upon Christmas Day who made lame beggars walk and blind men see."

Bob's voice was tremulous when he told them this, and trembled more when he said that Tiny Tim was growing strong and hearty.

His active little crutch was heard upon the floor, and back came Tiny Tim before another word was spoken, escorted by his brother and sister to his stool beside the fire; and while Bob, turning up his cuffs—as if, poor fellow, they were capable of being made more shabby—compounded some hot mixture in a jug with gin and lemons, and stirred it round and round, and put it on the hob to simmer, Master Peter and the two ubiquitous young Cratchits went to fetch the goose, with which they soon returned in high procession.

Such a bustle ensued that you might have thought a goose the rarest of all birds; a feathered phenomenon, to which a black swan was a matter of course—and in truth, it was something very like it in that house.

Mrs. Cratchit made the gravy (ready beforehand in a little saucepan) hissing hot; Master Peter mashed the potatoes with incredible vigor; Miss Belinda sweetened up the applesauce; Martha dusted the hot plates; Bob took Tiny Tim beside him in a tiny corner at the table; the two young Cratchits set chairs for everyone, not forgetting themselves, and, mounting guard upon their posts, crammed spoons into their mouths, lest they should shriek for goose before their turn came to be helped.

At last the dishes were set on, and grace was said. It was succeeded by a breathless pause, as Mrs. Cratchit, looking slowly all along the carving-knife, prepared to plunge it in the breast; but when she did, and when the long-expected gush of stuffing issued forth, one murmur of delight arose all round the board, and even Tiny Tim, excited by the two young Cratchits, beat on the table with the handle of his knife and feebly cried Hurrah!

There never was such a goose. Bob said he didn't believe there ever was such a goose cooked. Its tenderness and flavor, size and cheapness, were the themes of universal admiration. Eked out by applesauce and mashed potatoes, it was a sufficient dinner for the whole family; indeed, as Mrs. Cratchit said with great delight (surveying one small atom of a bone upon the dish), they hadn't ate it all at last! Yet every one had enough, and the youngest Cratchits, in particular, were steeped in sage and onion to the eyebrows! But now, the plates being changed by Miss Belinda, Mrs. Cratchit left the room alone—too nervous to bear witnesses to take the pudding up, and bring it in.

Suppose it should not be done enough! Suppose it should break in turning out! Suppose somebody should have got over the wall of the back-yard and stolen it, while they were merry with the goose—a supposition at which the two young Cratchits became livid! All sorts of horrors were supposed.

Hallo! A great deal of steam! the pudding was out of the copper. A smell like a washing-day! That was the cloth. A smell like an eating-house and a pastry-cook's next door to each other, with a laundress's next door to that! That was the pudding.

In a half a minute Mrs. Cratchit entered—flushed, but smiling proudly—with the pudding, like a speckled cannonball, so hard and firm, blazing in half of half-a-quartern of ignited brandy, and bedight with Christmas holly stuck into the top.

Oh, a wonderful pudding! Bob Cratchit said, and calmly, too, that he regarded it as the greatest success achieved by Mrs. Cratchit since their marriage. Mrs. Cratchit said that, now the weight was off her mind, she would confess she had her doubts about the quantity of flour. Everybody had something to say about it, but nobody said or thought it was at all a small pudding for a large family. It would have been flat heresy to do so. Any Cratchit would have blushed to hint at such a thing.

At last the dinner was all done, the cloth was cleared, the hearth swept, and the fire made up. The compound in the jug being tasted, and considered perfect, apples and oranges were put upon the table, and a shovelful of chestnuts on the fire. Then all the Cratchit family drew round the hearth in what Bob Cratchit called a circle, meaning half a one, and at Bob Cratchit's elbow stood the family display of glass. Two tumblers and a custard-cup without a handle. These held the hot stuff from the jug, however, as well as golden goblets would have done; and Bob served it out with beaming looks, while the chestnuts on the fire sputtered and cracked noisily. Then Bob proposed:

"A Merry Christmas to us all, my dears. God bless us!"

Which all the family re-echoed.

"God bless us every one!" said Tiny Tim, the last of all.

Christmas through a Child's Eyes

THE STORY OF SANTA CLAUS

Once upon a time, a man called Nicholas lived in Patara, a town in the East. Because he was very fond of children and was kind and generous to them, they came to think of him as their dear friend and their beloved saint. So it was that after a time the wonderful things he did were woven into a beautiful legend. You know that *Santa* means *Saint* and *Claus* stands for *Nicholas,* and that is how he came to be known as Santa Claus.

In Santa Claus's own town, Patara, lived a great lord who had three daughters. He was very poor, so poor that one day he was on the point of sending his daughters out to beg for food from his neighbors. But it happened that Saint Nicholas not long before had come into a fortune, and as he loved giving to those in need, he no sooner heard of the trouble the poor lord was in than he made up his mind to help him secretly. So he went to the nobleman's house at night, and as the moon shone out from behind a cloud, he saw an open window into which he threw a bag of gold, and with this timely gift the father was able to provide for his eldest daughter, so that she could be married. On another night Santa Claus set off with another bag of gold, and threw it in at the window, so the second daughter was provided for. But by this time, the father had grown eager to discover who the mysterious visitor could be, and next night he kept on the lookout. Then for the third time Santa Claus came with a bag of gold upon his back and pitched it in at the window. The old lord at once recognized his fellow townsman, and falling on his knees, cried out: "Oh! Nicholas, servant of God, why seek to hide yourself?"

Is it not wonderful to think that this was so long ago, sixteen hundred years, yet we still look for the secret coming of Santa Claus with his Christmas gifts? At first he was said to come on his own birthday, which is early in December, but after awhile, as was very natural with Christmas so near, the night of his coming was moved on in the calendar, and now we hang up our stockings to receive his gifts on Christmas Eve. In some countries children still put their shoes by the fireside on his birthday. In others they say it is the Christ-Kindlein or Christ Child who brings the gifts at Christmas-time. But it is always a surprise visit, and though it has happened so many hundreds of times, the hanging up of the Christmas stocking is still as great a delight as ever.

Author Unknown

The Sugarplum Tree

Eugene Field

Have you ever heard of the Sugarplum Tree?
'Tis a marvel of great renown!
It blooms on the shore of the Lollipop sea
In the garden of Shut-Eye Town;
The fruit that it bears is so wondrously sweet
(As those who have tasted it say)
That good little children have only to eat
Of that fruit to be happy next day.

When you've got to the tree, you would have a hard time
To capture the fruit which I sing;
The tree is so tall that no person could climb
To the boughs where the sugarplums swing!
But up in that tree sits a chocolate cat,
And a gingerbread dog prowls below—
And this is the way you contrive to get at
Those sugarplums tempting you so:

You say but the word to that gingerbread dog
And he barks with such terrible zest
That the chocolate cat is at once all agog,
As her swelling proportions attest.
And the chocolate cat goes cavorting around
From this leafy limb unto that,
And the sugarplums tumble, of course, to the ground—
Hurrah for that chocolate cat!

There are marshmallows, gumdrops, and peppermint canes,
With stripings of scarlet or gold,
And you carry away of the treasure that rains
As much as your apron can hold!
So come, little child, cuddle closer to me
In your dainty white nightcap and gown,
And I'll rock you away to that Sugarplum Tree
In the garden of Shut-Eye Town.

From POEMS OF CHILDHOOD by Eugene Field (Charles Scribner's Sons).

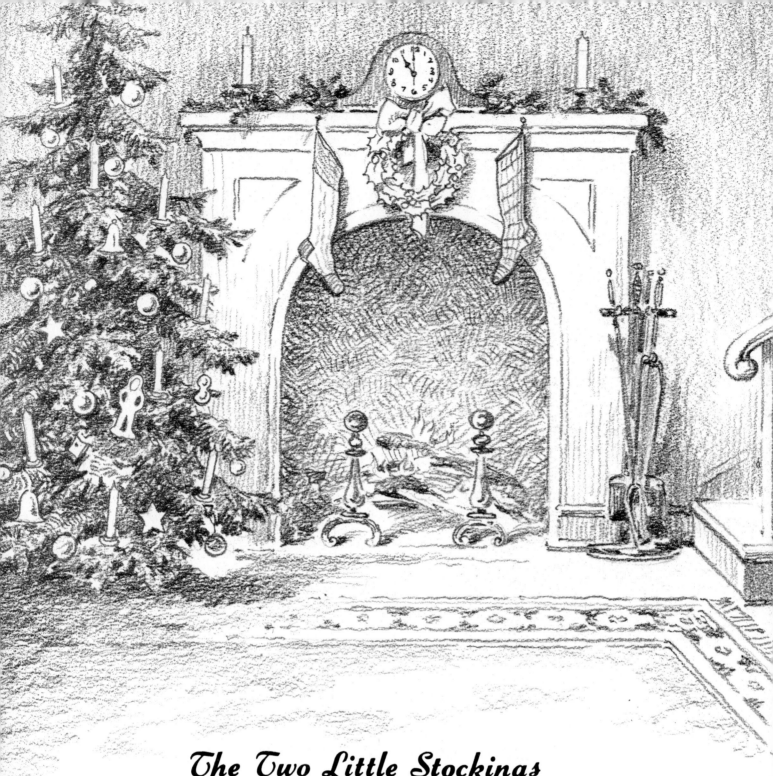

The Two Little Stockings

R. G. Anthony

Two little stockings,
   As clean as could be,
Hung near the staircase
   For Santa to see.

Said one little stocking,
   "What time will he come
And will he bring Sandra
   A pretty red drum?"

The other small stocking,
   Put up by Michele,
Replied in a whisper,
   "I really can't tell

"Because it's the very
   First Christmas for me
So we must be patient
   And see what we'll see."

The first little stocking
   Said, "I'll stay awake.
When Santa comes over
   To fill me, I'll make

"Myself a bit bigger
   by stretching my thread."
"Yes, then you will hold more,"
   Michele's stocking said.

Two little stockings,
    Who vowed they would keep
Their eyes on old Santa,
    Were soon fast asleep.

The clock kept on ticking
    And then it was dawn.
Sandra's small stocking
    Awoke with a yawn.

"Oh dear, how my back aches,"
    It said to its friend.
"I'm so stiff and heavy
    That I cannot bend!"

And then it discovered
    A huge sugar cane
And lots of hard candies
    Were causing the pain.

Michele's little stocking
    Said, "I feel like you.
What's worse, we were sleeping
    When Santa came through."

"*Oh hush! I hear voices,*"
    The other one said,
"*So look wise and happy*
    And lift up your head."

Two little children
    Appeared with a shout
And rushed to their stockings
    To pull the sweets out.

"*To think we were sleeping*
    When Santa Claus came!"
Michele said to Sandra,
    Who nodded in shame.

"If only our stockings
    Could talk!" Sandra said.
"They must have seen Santa
    While we were in bed."

And what of the stockings,
    Now empty and meek?
Oh, they were just stockings
    And stockings don't speak!

The Cookie Jar Elf

Harold C. Bingman

Once there was a gnome, a quaint little elf,
Who lived in a cookie jar up on a shelf,
In Santa Claus' kitchen, way up where it's cold,
And on each Christmas Eve, this story is told.

Although he's no part of the regular crew
Who gets presents ready for me and for you,
His job is important, as Santa has said,
For he makes the snow for old Santa Claus' sled.

When the sled is all loaded and ready to go,
He turns on the blower that makes the winds blow;
Then cuts in the cold, and the white flakes sift down,
Till a blanket of white lies on village and town.

Then when reindeer and friends are all ready to fly,
He sets the stars out in the Christmas Eve sky;
Then lights up the moon, so their path will be bright
And no house will be missed on this most special night.

Then the frost fairies sing, and they clasp hands in glee
As Santa goes flying o'er land and o'er sea;
While back at the North Pole, the cookie jar gnome
Keeps the big moon a-glowing, and a warm fire at home

And when Santa returns from his world-wide cruise,
He takes off his red suit, removes his wet shoes;
Pulls up a soft chair, tired, he just wants to sit
And puff on the pipe that his gnome friend has lit.

Outside the wind moans round the mountains of ice,
And whistles down chimney, but inside it's nice,
While the Northern Lights flame the cold frosty air,
Old Santa is snuggled deep down in his chair.

As the white flakes sift down from the darkening skies,
From the kitchen there comes the aroma of pies,
And cookies and biscuits so fluffy and airy;
While asleep by the fire is Kris Kringle and fairy.

Then the gnome wakens up and turns off the blower,
Cuts down the cold so the flakes fall much slower,
And as Christmas day dawns, streaks of blue and of gold —
The snow storm is over, though the air is still cold.

Then the cookie jar elf rushes off to the steeple,
And tolls on the bells to awaken the people;
While in cities and hamlets, both far and both near,
The glad news rings out, Christmas finally is here.

Then the children all jump from the warmth of their bed,
And rush for the presents from Santa Claus' sled;
The candies and nuts and the cookies galore,
And the glittering toys strewn round the floor.

Now this is the story of the Santa Claus gnome
Who lives at the North Pole in Santa Claus' home;
Though we don't know his name, we know what he'll do
When Christmas comes round, just for me and for you.

The Life of Santa Claus

Florence Granquist Ray

Deep in the country of snows up and down,
Far in the northland — away from a town,
Santa's old house of remarkable charm,
Lies in the snowdrifts that cover his farm.

All of the windows you see in the night,
Are bordered with snow and shining with light.
All through the evenings, and all through the year,
The light you can see, and the noise you can hear.

Busy old Santa, so happy and wise,
Is making new toys for a Christmas surprise..
Sawing and pounding and painting away,
Colorful things for the next Christmas Day.

Out of the chimney, the smoke rises high,
Straight through the air to the stars in the sky;
Up from the fireplace crackling and warm,
Out in the cold . . . and the wind . . . and the storm.

Dear Mrs. Santa is busy within,
Reading to Santa the letters for him;
Cooking and sewing and lending a hand,
Dressing new dolls for the girls of the land;

Knitting their sweaters and curling their hair,
Tying their bonnets and slippers to wear;
Rocking them softly to sleep with a song,
Thoughtfully sending their blankets along.

Just a short way from the big kitchen door,
Stands the old barn with a rough wooden floor . . .
Snuggled against a white hillside of snow,
Cozy and warm for the reindeer, you know.

Day after day, every morning and night,
Santa goes out with a lantern for light,
Pumping the water for all of the deer,
Feeding them hay from the loft that is near.

Patting them gently . . . each one in his stall,
Jingling the sleighbells that hang on the wall,
Calling their names; for they listen, and know
Santa will take them out in the snow.

Back to the barn go the reindeer once more.
Santa has finished his everyday chore;
Up to the house and right on with his work,
(Never a moment would Santa Claus shirk.)

All through the day, and far into the night,
Year after year and with all of his might,
Santa is busy — as busy can be
Making good presents for you and for me.

Deep in the country of snows up and down,
Far in the Northland — is Santa Claus town.

THE JUGGLER
OF NOTRE DAME

Anatole France

In the days when the world was young, there lived in France a man of no importance. Everyone said he was a man of no importance, and he firmly believed this himself. For he was just a poor traveling juggler, who could not read or write, who went about from town to town following the little country fairs, and performing his tricks for a few pennies a day. His name was Barnaby.

When the weather was beautiful, and people were strolling about the streets, this juggler would find a clear space in the Village Square, spread a strip of old carpet out on the cobblestones, and on it he would perform his tricks for children and grown-ups alike. Now Barnaby, although he knew he was a man of no importance, was an amazing juggler.

First he would only balance a tin plate on the tip of his nose. But when the crowd had collected, he would stand on his hands and juggle six copper balls in the air at the same time, catching them with his feet. And sometimes, when he would juggle twelve sharp knives in the air, the villagers would be so delighted that a rain of pennies would fall on his strip of carpet. And when his day's work was over, and he was wearily resting his aching muscles, Barnaby would collect the pennies in his hat, kneel down reverently and thank God for the gift.

Always the people would laugh at his simplicity and everyone would agree that Barnaby would never amount to anything. But all this is about the happy days in Barnaby's life. The springtime days when people were willing to toss a penny to a poor juggler. When winter came, Barnaby had to wrap his juggling equipment in the carpet, and trudge along the roads begging a night's lodging in farmers' barns, or entertaining the servants of some rich nobleman to earn a meal. And Barnaby never thought of complaining – he knew that the winter and the rains were as necessary as the spring sunshine, and he accepted his lot; "for how," Barnaby would say to himself as he trudged along, "could such an ignorant fellow as myself hope for anything better."

And one year in France there was a terrible winter. It began to rain in October and there was hardly a blue sky to be seen by the end of November. And on an evening in early December at the end of a dreary, wet day, as Barnaby trudged along a country road, sad and bent, carrying under his arm the golden balls and knives wrapped up in his old carpet, he met a Monk. Riding a fine white mule, dressed in warm clothes, well-fed and comfortable, the Monk smiled at the sight of Barnaby and called to him: "It's going to be cold before morning .... how would you like to spend the night at the monastery?"

And that night Barnaby found himself seated at the great candle-lit dining hall of the Monastery. Although he sat at the bottom of the long table, together with the servants and beggars, Barnaby thought he had never seen such a wonderful place in his life. The shining faces of fifty Monks relaxing after this day of work and prayer.

Barnaby did not dare to suggest that he should perform his tricks as they would be sacrilege before such men, but as he ate and drank more than he had ever had at a meal for years, a great resolution came over him. Although it made him tremble at his own boldness, as the meal ended, Barnaby suddenly arose, ran around the table down to where the Lordly Abbot sat at the head, and sank to his knees: "Father .... grant my prayer! Let me stay in this wonderful place and work for you! I cannot hope to become one of you, I am too ignorant .... but let me work in the kitchen and the fields, and worship with you in the Chapel!"

The Monk who had met Barnaby on the road turned to the Abbot: "This is a good man, simple and pure of heart." So the Abbot nodded, and Barnaby that night put his juggling equipment under a cot in his own cubicle, and decided that never again would he go back to his old profession.

And in the days that followed, everyone smiled at the eager way he scrubbed the floors and labored throughout the buildings; and everyone smiled at his simplicity. As for Barnaby his face shone with happiness from morning until night.

Until two weeks before Christmas . . . . then Barnaby's joy suddenly turned to misery . For around him he saw every man preparing a wonderful gift to place in the Chapel on Christmas . Brother Maurice , who had the art of illuminating copies of the Bible . And Brother Marbode was completing a marvelous statue of Christ ; Brother Ambrose , who wrote music , and had completed scoring a great hymn to be played on the organ during Christmas services.

All about Barnaby , those educated , trained artists followed their work . . . . each one of them readying a beautiful gift to dedicate to God on Christmas day . And what about Barnaby ? — he could do nothing . "I am but a rough man , unskilled in the arts , and I can write no book , offer no painting or statue or poem . . . . alas . . . . I have no talent , I have no gift worthy of the day !"

To Barnaby sank deep into sadness and despair . Christmas day came . . . . and the chapel was resplendent with the gifts of the Brothers . . . . the giant organ rang with the new music ; the choir sang the Chorales ; the candles glittered around the great new statue . And Barnaby was not there . . . . he was in his tiny cubicle , praying forgiveness for having no gift to offer .

Then a strange thing happened . On the evening of Christmas day , when the Chapel should have been deserted , one of the Monks came running white-faced and panting with exertion into the private office of the Abbot . He threw open the door without knocking , seized the Abbot by the arms . "Father . . . . a frightful thing is happening . . . . the most terrible sacrilege ever to take place is going on right in our own chapel ! Come !"

Together the two portly men ran down the corridors , burst through a door , and came out on the balcony at the rear of the chapel . The Monk pointed down toward the altar . The Abbot looked , turned ashen in color . "He is mad !"

For down below , in front of the altar , was Barnaby . He had spread out his strip of carpet , and kneeling reverently upon it, was actually juggling in the air twelve golden balls! He was giving his old performance.... and giving it beautifully.... his bright knives .... the shining balls, the tin plate balanced on the tip of his nose. And on his face was a look of adoration and joy.

We must seize him at once," cried the Abbot, and turned for the door. But at that moment a light filled the church .... a brilliant beam of light coming directly from the altar, and .... both the Monks sank to their knees.

For as Barnaby knelt exhausted on his carpet, they saw the Statue of the Virgin Mary move; she came down from her pedestal, and coming to where Barnaby knelt, she took the blue hem of her robe and touched it to his forehead, gently drying the perspiration that glistened there. Then the light dimmed. And up in the choir-balcony the Monk looked at his superior: "God accepted the only gift he had to make."

And the Abbot slowly nodded:

Blessed are the simple in heart.... for they shall see God."

This old favorite has been universally loved by people of all faiths for its warm portrayal of the spirit that is Christmas. It is presented here with the heartfelt hope that, whatever your belief, you will have found in its message added meaning for your celebration of the birth of the Son of God.

Reprinted by permission of Dodd, Mead & Company. From their book: MOTHER OF PEARL.

The Little
Match Girl

A long, long time ago—on a bitter cold New Year's eve—a poor little girl with bare feet was trudging along through the cold deep snow.

Yes, her feet were bare—because she had no real shoes—and the large slippers some one had given her had been lost when she ran to get out of the way of a cart—and a naughty boy ran away with one of them.

So she was walking in the bitter, bitter cold snow and her poor little bare feet were red and blue with cold.

In her apron she was carrying a lot of matches that she was trying to sell for a penny a box.

No one had bought any from her all day long —and the poor little thing was shivering and hungry—but she was afraid to go home—because her cruel foster father would beat her— for she had not sold even a half-penny of matches all day long.

She looked into the bright cheerful windows of homes as she walked by—everyone seemed so warm and comfortable and happy —everyone except the poor little match girl.

She saw a beautiful trimmed Christmas tree in one—from another came the tempting aroma of roast goose—and she was so very hungry.

It was getting colder—and snowing harder— and it was now real dark—when she huddled in a corner between two buildings to try to keep warm.

She took one little match from a box and lit it to warm her frozen fingers. How brightly it sputtered—in its light she seemed to see a big warm stove—how warm and cozy it was—but when the match burned out—the stove disappeared—and she was colder than ever.

She struck a second match—and before her was a big table—with glistening white table

cloth—there was a huge roast duck—and apples—and cake and warm milk—and she was so happy because she was so terribly hungry. Then just when she was reaching for the roast duck—the match burned out—and, then she was colder and more hungry than ever.

She lighted another match—and lo!—there was the most beautiful Christmas tree she had ever seen—full of shiny toys and sparkling candles, candies and everything nice.

The beautiful candles rose higher and higher—until they were only stars in the sky—then one of them fell.

"That falling star means some one is dying" she said to herself—"my dear grandmother used to tell me that."

She quickly lit another match—and another —then a whole hand full—and right in the bright glow—so dazzling and bright, and so kind and loving stood her dear old grandmother with outstretched arms.

"Grandmother!" she cried—"please take me with you! I know you will go away when the match burns out—just like the roast goose and the warm stove and the Christmas tree did."

She quickly lighted the whole box of matches —because she did not want her grandmother to go. The matches burned with a blaze that was as light as day—her grandmother had never seemed so beautiful—and as she took the poor little match girl in her arms she flew up with her in brightness and joy, high, so very high—and there was no cold and no hunger—and no sorrow—and—no matches to sell—for they were in heaven.

In the morning, people passed by and saw the poor little girl still huddled between the buildings, with burned matches about her.

Adapted from
HANS CHRISTIAN ANDERSEN

LITTLE BOY BLUE

Eugene Field

The little toy dog is covered with dust,
But sturdy and staunch he stands;
And the little toy soldier is red with rust,
And his musket molds in his hands.

Time was when the little toy dog was new
And the soldier was passing fair,
And that was the time when our Little Boy Blue
Kissed them and put them there.

*"Now, don't you go till I come," he said,
"And don't you make any noise!"
So toddling off to his trundle-bed
He dreamed of the pretty toys.*

*And as he was dreaming, an angel song
Awakened our Little Boy Blue . . .
Oh, the years are many, the years are long,
But the little toy friends are true.*

Aye, faithful to Little Boy Blue they stand,
Each in the same old place,
Awaiting the touch of a little hand
And the smile of a little face.

And they wonder, as waiting these long years through,
In the dust of that little chair,
What has become of our Little Boy Blue
Since he kissed them and put them there.

From A LITTLE BOOK OF WESTERN VERSE by Eugene Field (Charles Scribner's Sons 1889).

Dear Santa

I guess you know
It's the time of the year
When everyone's happy
And sending good cheer.

When you come to our house,
There you will see
Two bright red stockings,
Lights and a tree.

In the kitchen,
Cake and candy, too,
With a note that says,
"Just for you!"

I've been a good girl,
Waiting for you.
PS Bring something for
My sister, too!

Marcella Denise Simon

A Rest for Santa

You must be tired, Santa,
You've worked the whole night through;
So sit and rest a moment
And eat a little, too.

I made the cookies specially
And surely hope you'll find
That each and every one of them
Is quite your favorite kind.

And when you lift your pack again
And hurry on your way,
Take with you all our wishes
For a happy Christmas Day.

Virginia Blanck Moore

The Night Before Christmas

Clement Clarke Moore
(1779-1863)

'Twas the night before Christmas, when all through the house
Not a creature was stirring, not even a mouse;
The stockings were hung by the chimney with care,
In hopes that St. Nicholas soon would be there.

The children were nestled all snug in their beds,
While visions of sugar-plums danced in their heads;
And Mamma in her 'kerchief, and I in my cap,
Had just settled our brains for a long winter's nap.

When out on the lawn there arose such a clatter,
I sprang from my bed to see what was the matter.
Away to the window I flew like a flash,
Tore open the shutters and threw up the sash.

The moon on the breast of the new-fallen snow
Gave a lustre of mid-day to objects below,
When, what to my wondering eyes did appear,
But a miniature sleigh, and eight tiny reindeer.

With a little old driver, so lively and quick,
I knew in a moment it must be St. Nick.
More rapid than eagles his coursers they came,
And he whistled, and shouted, and called them by name.

"Now, Dasher! now, Dancer! now, Prancer and Vixen!
On, Comet! on, Cupid! on, Donner and Blitzen!
To the top of the porch! to the top of the wall!
Now dash away! dash away! dash away all!"

As dry leaves that before the wild hurricane fly,
When they meet with an obstacle, mount to the sky,
So up to the house-top the coursers they flew,
With the sleigh full of Toys, and St. Nicholas too.

And then, in a twinkling, I heard on the roof
The prancing and pawing of each little hoof.
As I drew in my head, and was turning around,
Down the chimney St. Nicholas came with a bound.

He was dressed all in fur, from his head to his foot,
And his clothes were all tarnished with ashes and soot;
A bundle of Toys he had flung on his back,
And he looked like a peddler just opening his pack.

His eyes— how they twinkled! his dimples, how merry!
His cheeks were like roses, his nose like a cherry!
His droll little mouth was drawn up like a bow,
And the beard on his chin was as white as the snow.

The stump of a pipe he held tight to his teeth,
And the smoke it encircled his head like a wreath;
He had a broad face and a little round belly,
That shook when he laughed, like a bowl full of jelly.

He was chubby and plump, a right jolly old elf,
And I laughed when I saw him, in spite of myself;
A wink of his eye and a twist of his head
Soon gave me to know I had nothing to dread.

He spoke not a word, but went straight to his work,
And filled all the stockings; then turned with a jerk,
And laying his finger aside of his nose,
And giving a nod, up the chimney he rose.

He sprang to his sleigh, to his team gave a whistle,
And away they all flew like the down of a thistle.
But I heard him exclaim ere he drove out of sight,
"Happy Christmas to all . . . and to all a goodnight!"

An Old-Fashioned Christmas

Christmas Fantasy

Dianne McGowan

"The children were nestled all snug in their beds,
While visions of sugar plums danced in their heads . . . "

Now, Clement Clarke Moore wrote these words long ago
But even today they are still really so.
For Christmas is fantasy when children dream
Of Santa Claus, reindeer and presents that gleam.

It's poetry, romance, and all sorts of things
And dreaming of everything Santa Claus brings.
So after the children have said their good-nights,
They all begin dreaming of Christmas delights.

Now, once they're in dreamland they'll probably view
The same sort of things that were seen once by you.
There're red poinsettias and sparkly white snow;
And candy cane chimneys wherever they go.

There're lollypop stars and stuffed animals, too;
There're all kinds of dolls and a make-believe zoo;
A tree trimmed with popcorn; a tree trimmed with candy;
And somewhere in sight is a bike that's just dandy.

There're gingerbread men and a gingerbread house;
A big tall giraffe and a wee tiny mouse;
There're soldiers and drums and a red rocking chair . . .
It's all so amazing, the things that are there.

And Santa is working so hard in his shop;
He's having such fun that he simply won't stop.
There're angels and teddy bears, little green elves,
And all sorts of wonderful toys on the shelves.

Yes, Christmas is magic and fantasy, too;
It's knowing that Santa is coming to you.
It's going to bed and then closing your eyes
And finding yourself in a dreamland surprise.

Toys for Your Delight

THE MENAGERIE IS COMING RIGHT TO Your House!

(*just as soon as you send for it,*)

TO STAY WITH YOU

One, Two, Three Years,

and longer if you don't abuse the Animals.

(*They are very strong, and will keep so, without Eating anything either, if you treat them fairly.*)

Woodcut of a Christmas advertisement, courtesy The Bettmann Archive.

Working with sparse materials and simple hand tools, the country's pioneer toymakers fashioned playthings that amused generations of children. Many of these charming old toys were made at home—a cabinetmaker might carve a horse and rider, farmyard animal or some other toy for his own children or those of his neighbors—or by folk artisans, itinerants who roamed from place to place peddling and earning a living as best they could. Today many of these simple toys reside in museums and restorations, and delight collectors, who pay dearly for the best specimens.

Toy dolls are as old as civilization; examples exist from ancient Greece, and there are records of rag dolls being enjoyed in Europe as early as the ninth century. Dolls were introduced to the American Indians by colonists who arrived during the reign of Queen Elizabeth.

Early settlers in America used ingenious materials to fashion dolls for their own children. The classic rag doll used up scraps of material left over from making the family's clothing. Because of the hard wear these fabric dolls absorbed, few really early examples survive, but we know from contemporary records that they were made. Another favorite was the bedpost doll, so named because its head was a circular ball of wood that looked for all the world like a bedpost; some are alleged to have come from discarded bedposts destined for the woodpile. Brush and paint provided facial features, some cloth and rags a body. Makers with sculptural skills went a step further and gouged out a bas-relief nose. Jointed dolls in the likenesses of soldiers, Indians and people in everyday dress were made of tin and thin wood well before the Revolution. By bending the movable arms, legs, lower torso and head, the dolls could assume any number of positions. A wonderful example of a pre-Revolutionary tin doll is included in a collection at the Jeremiah Lee House in Marblehead, Massachusetts. A child's imagination turned dolls made of peanuts strung together, cornhusks, even turkey wishbones, into cherished companions.

Reprinted with permission of the publisher, from EARLY AMERICAN LIFE magazine, December 1975.

By the beginning of the nineteenth century, the doll was thoroughly established as a plaything—the child of the child—and manufacturers began to realize that it had great potential as an industry. Dollmakers in Germany, England, and France used wax, papier maché, china, and bisque to produce a great variety of dolls, complete with wardrobes and accessories in the latest modes. Even after the age of industrialization, when American toy factories sprang up, most dolls sold in this country bore heads imported from Europe, where a more established toy industry was able to produce them more easily and cheaply.

In addition to dolls, early toymakers produced a great variety of other games and playthings. Most were made of wood, carved or merely saw-cut, depending on the skill of the maker, and were usually painted, although the paint may now be worn away, as most were given only one coat. On occasion, antique-hunters find toys that were repainted at a later date; no matter how good the repainting, they are always worth less than specimens with at least some of the original paint.

Wood is a versatile material. Out of it came everything from tiny carved "black sheep," which itinerants sold for a penny, to scale-model milk-wagons, complete with horses and drivers, with milkcans of carved wood painted in silver gilt. Movable toys were made by rigging them with string or bands of India rubber. One of the most popular street corner toys of the late nineteenth century was a saw-cut, brightly colored monkey suspended from a piece of twine between two sticks. When the sticks were squeezed, the monkey tumbled over the twine like a circus acrobat. The twine to which the figure was attached had a twist in it; when it was pulled taut the monkey danced.

Papier mache doll with glass eyes, courtesy The Bettmann Archive.

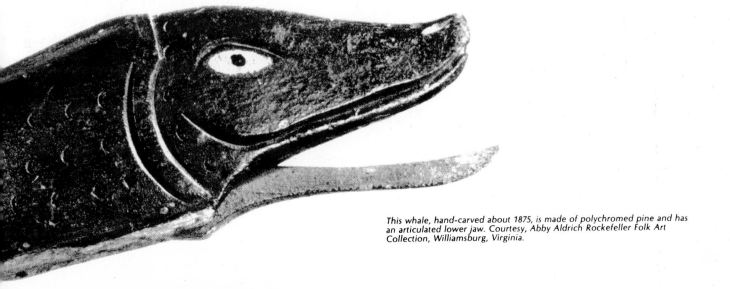

This whale, hand-carved about 1875, is made of polychromed pine and has an articulated lower jaw. Courtesy, Abby Aldrich Rockefeller Folk Art Collection, Williamsburg, Virginia.

To add motion to wooden toys, wheels were added, attached either from axles running between the toy's front and rear legs or on wooden platforms to which the toy was glued or nailed. Giraffes, goats, cows, bisons and hippos were all made into "four-wheelers." Horses on wheels, scaled for two- and three-years-old riders, were common during the nineteenth century. For variety the animal was sometimes a cow, donkey or even a huge chicken. In the Bella Landauer collection in the New York Historical Society is a large elephant on wheels; painted jet black, it must have delighted some youngster in the 1850s.

Any number of experiments were tried to catch the fancies of children and their parents. An enterprising toymaker in Lebanon County, Pennsylvania, who most likely had never seen a kangaroo in his life, carved a kangaroo doll. He didn't skimp; the model is a full 47½ inches long and is now the joy of a private collector. About 1870, an anonymous New England toymaker created a balancing toy that illustrates the

ingenuity of early designers. Made of polychromed wood and metal, it is a man in a tall silk hat, complete with a mustache and goatee, standing on a tall pedestal. He holds in his outstretched arms a bent wire with a wooden ball at each end. Even when correctly balanced, he sways from one side to the other, but the wooden balls keep him from toppling over. The balancing

This balancing man was made in the last quarter of the nineteenth century by an unknown carver. It is made of polychromed wood. Courtesy, Abby Aldrich Rockefeller Folk Art Collection, Williamsburg, Virginia.

man" is now in the Abby Aldrich Rockefell Art Collection. Many similar balancing toy imported from Europe during the latter par nineteenth century.

Because they were a chore to construct, "d dolls" were somewhat less common than ba toys. Many collectors think of dancing d wind-ups of fairly recent vintage, those whic clockwork motors in their bases. Their pr sors, wooden dolls a foot or less in height and in the round, managed to dance without m The arms—made of one piece, and the legs— of two pieces, were joined to the body loose pins, so that with the least vibration, th came animated. The doll was then attac a wire that suspended it over a woode By gently tapping the wire, the doll c and clattered.

"Pecking hens" (or turkey greatly amusing. The s painted birds were r ed to a board weighted lum h from it. the pen was g swing bird's

bobbed up and down in a pecking motion the pendulum came to a stop.

Often designed to represent the various fessions, whirligigs have certain scientific tones as well. They are wooden figures, usu in human form, with large arms in the sha paddles. Mounted, or simply held in the h out of doors, the arms are caug the wind and spin lik

wheel. By seeing which way the whirligig spins,
the wind's direction is revealed. The speed of its
running gives a rough idea of wind velocity. Good,
well-preserved whirligigs are scarce, and many of
the better examples are in museums as they deserve
to be.

Stationary wooden toys flourished along with the
movable, and among the most appealing of these are
Noah's arks, houses mounted on rafts built of wood
and painted, with a menagerie of animals—in dupli-
cate, of course, true to the Old Testament account.
Usually the ark's roof lifted up like a chest lid, and
the animals could be stored inside. The size of the
ark and the number of figures it contained varied.
Small ones might comprise no more than common
barnyard animals, with which the children would be
familiar. With larger arks, many carved by pro-
fessionals both in the United States and in Europe,
came more variety, although the figures were not
necessarily bigger. Some contained as many as three
dozen pairs of animals. In addition to domestic
animals, toy designers produced a fanciful jungle of

elephants, giraffes, water buffalo, rhinos, hippos
and monkeys, none of which were they ever likely to
have seen in the flesh. Carvings of exotic animals
were based on drawings and paintings by artists who
probably never saw the animals either, but no child
was ever known to complain about the inaccuracy.

In the collector's market, the value of antique toys
depends upon age, uniqueness and workmanship.
Because of the rough handling toys have always
received, allowances are made for condition. Except
for mechanical banks, cast-iron fire engines, and
motor trains, carved wooden toys are usually the
most highly valued, being original works of art that
were not cast from molds or otherwise
mass-duplicated.

William Rodger

*Above: Children playing with hoops, a favorite toy of the 1930s.
Courtesy, The Bettmann Archive.*

*Opposite: 17th century hobbyhorse brought to the Colonies by the
Dutch. Courtesy, The Bettmann Archive.*

81

Christmas Memory Lane

by Erwin L. Hess

CHRISTMAS IS A TIME OF THE YEAR WHEN WE THINK OF OUR OLD, CHILDHOOD NEIGHBORHOOD, OUR OWN LITTLE WORLD OF THE PAST...NOW JUST A MEMORY. THE FEEL OF NEW SNOW AT CHRISTMASTIME TAKES US BACK TO A SPARKLING NIGHT OF YESTERYEAR ....

....WHEN THE SNO[W] SQUEAKED AND MEW[ED] BENEATH OUR FEE[T] AS WE TRUDGED AL[ONG] THE ROAD WHERE SLEIGHS, BOBSLED[S] AND CUTTERS HA[D] MADE WALKING EASIER. AS OUR ME[RRY] THOUGHTS CONTIN[UE] TO DRIFT FURTHER BACK TO CHRISTMA[S] OF YESTERYEAR, [A] CONGLOMERATION [OF] OTHER MEMORIES PULLS US BACK IN[TO] THE PAST. EASILY AND SWIFTLY WE FIND OURSELVES [NO] LONGER TRUDGING BUT SCAMPERING DOWN .....

Memory Lan[e]

AND, ...

ONCE WE ARE ON MEMORY LANE, IT'S EASY FOR US TO POKE THROUGH THE HAZE WHICH HAS SHROUDED THE DIM PAST FROM THE BRIGHT PRESENT....AND, PLOP! WE ARE RIGHT DAB-SMACK INTO A CHRISTMAS YESTERYEAR! PLEASANTRIES OF OLD AGAIN SURROUND US. OF COURSE, THEY'RE ONLY MERRY MEMORIES....

YES, IN THOSE DAYS CHRISTMASTIME WAS MORE SIMPLE AND THE WORLD AROUND US WAS SO STILL ....

AT NIGHT, TOO; AND SO DARK AND QUIET THAT THE ONLY LIGHT IT WERE THE LITTLE GOLDEN FLAMES OF CANDLES AND THE LITTI SILVER FLAMES OF STARS, ALMOST LIKE THAT FIRST SILENT NIGHT.

WHEN THE CHRIST CHILD WAS BORN!

THAT PARTICULAR CHRISTMAS EV IN OUR OLD NEIGHBORHOOD WAS ALMOST SUCH A SILENT NIGHT ...

AT FIRST IT WASN'T... BUT, BY THE MINUTE IT WAS GETTING QUIETER; NEARING SILENCE. THE CHURCH WINDOWS WERE GLOWING IN WARM COLORS AND THE BELLS WERE STILL!

EARLIER, THE CHURCH BELLS RANG. THOSE BELLS DID NOT SOUND LIKE THE SUNDAY BELLS. THEY WERE EXCITED AND YOUNG AND JUBILANT! WE WALKED HOMEWARD....

FAINTLY WE COULD STILL HEAR THE PLEASANT SOUNDS OF YULETIDE GAIETY COMING FROM THE SHOPPING CENTER WE LEFT BEHIND.....

IT WAS A HAPPY HUBBUB, FOLKS TAKING CARE OF LITTLE THINGS, LIKE WE DID, IN PREPARATION FOR THE MORNING, WITH ITS MERRY EXCITEMENT AND CHURCH SERVICE.

AS WE REACHED OUR NEIGHBORHOOD,...

'TWAS INDEED PEACE, CONTENTMENT AND GENUINE FRIENDLINESS _ THE REAL CHRISTMAS SPIRIT. THE FRAGRANT ODOR OF BURNING WOOD AND BALSAM MINGLED DELICIOUSLY WITH THE SMELL OF COFFEE, FOR A POT OF IT ALWAYS BREWED _ READY FOR ANYONE WHO WOULD STOP BY.....

YES, THOSE NEIGHBORS WERE SO GOOD...AND THE OLD NEIGHBORHOOD WAS SO NICE...AND THE ENTIRE SURROUNDINGS WERE SO PLEASANT.

THERE WERE SNOWY STRE... DIMLY LIGHT... WITH THE CORN... LAMPS.......A... DARK BUNDLE... OF PEOPLE SA... IN CUTTERS A... THEY DASHED... SMOOTHLY DO... THE STREET... AND THERE W... ITS OLD-FASHI... STORES.....O... OF THEM MAM... WENT TO....V... WENT WITH HE... 'TWAS A NICE... PLACE. ESPECI... NICE WERE TH... JARS FULL OF... COLORED CAND... ON THE COUNT...

'TWAS LIKE THAT AT OUR HOUSE, TOO!

THAT WAS THE STORE WE TRUDGED TO ON THAT SPARKLING NIGHT OF YESTERYEAR...A CHRISTMAS EVE WE REMEMBER DISTINCTLY.

THE STORE WE WENT TO WAS ON A BUSY STREET, NOT FAR FROM OUR NEIGHBORHOOD! THERE WAS THE HEADY SMELL OF THE PONDEROUS OLD RED COFFEE GRINDER _ THE HEAVY AROMA OF SPICES IN OPEN BINS _ THE FRAGRANCE OF GINGER AND CINNAMON AND OVERHEAD HUNG PAPER BAGS ON HOOKS AND LANTERNS AND MITTENS AND WHAT NOT. BEST OF ALL, THE GROCER GAVE US A SACK OF PEPPERMINT.... *and*...

HEN... AS AN ADDED TREAT FOR
HRISTMAS, HE SEARCHED THE
URKY BRINE OF A YAWNING
ARREL TO BRING FORTH SOME
IG DILL PICKLES, FOR US, ON A
ONG WOODEN LADLE. EVEN ON
HRISTMAS EVE A PICKLE TASTED
OOD! OUT ON THE BUSY STREET
ERE MANY PEOPLE.... BUSY, TOO!

WE LEFT THE STORE! OUTSIDE,
THE AIR CRACKED WITH THE
BELOW-ZERO FROST. EVERY-
THING WAS A PICTURE OF SILVER
FROST. LIGHTS FROM THE STORE
WINDOWS GLINTED YELLOW ON
THE SNOW. OUR NOSES WERE
GETTING COLORFUL, TOO..... A
CHERRY RED! IT WAS A VERY
BEAUTIFUL CHRISTMAS EVE,
INCREDIBLE HAPPINESS WAS
HEAPED UPON THAT LOVABLE
OLD-FASHIONED COMMUNITY
WITH ITS EASYGOING SPIRITS
AND ITS SIMPLE DELIGHTS.
SLEIGHBELLS MADE THE AIR
DANCE! A JOLLY MAN SOLD
HOT CHESTNUTS AND LAMP-
LIGHTS FLICKERED. THERE
WAS SOMETHING RICH ABOUT
THAT OLD-TIME SIMPLICITY.

'TWAS ALMOST SILENT. NOW AND THEN A BOB-SLED OR A CUTTER PASSED, ITS HARNESS JINGLING AND WE HEARD GOOD PEOPLE SINGING HYMNS ......

and then, ...

'TWAS SILENT!....A WONDERFUL CHRISTMAS EVE! WE REACHED HOME. THE LIGHT IN THE KITCHEN WAS WARMINGLY INVITING. THE WOODSHED DOOR, WHICH HAD BEEN LOCKED, WAS OPEN ... WE NOTICED IT!

WEBS OF SMOKE SPU[N] TOWARD THE STARS FROM THE CHIMNEYS INTO THE KITCHEN WE TRAMPLED, GLAD TO BE IN IT AGAIN! THE SENSE OF BEING SHUT IN FROM THE WORLD WAS SUCH A DELIGHTFUL FEELING. WE HAD NOTHING AGAINST THE WORLD, SO BEAUTIFUL 'TWAS OUTSIDE ...BUT OUR CHERRY-RED NOSES AND FROZEN TOES HAD SOMETHING AGAINST IT .... JUST TEMPORARILY!

ONCE IN THE WARM SNUGNESS OF THE HOUSE, WE DISCOVERED THAT THE PARLOR DOOR WAS LOCKED! THAT MEANT PAPA HAD A CHRISTMAS TREE IN THE WOODSHED! AND HE WAS TRIMMING IT! WE WERE CONVINCED WHEN WE HEARD ORNAMENTS FALL!

WE CANNOT DESCRIBE WHAT TOOK PLACE IN THE PARLOR BECAUSE WE DIDN'T SEE IT! WE TRIED TO LINGER IN THE KITCHEN WHERE MAMA MADE GOODIES, DELICIOUS ENOUGH TO MAKE A DICTIONARY LOOK BLANK WHEN WE TRIED TO FIND WORDS TO DESCRIBE THE FLAVORS... *BUT,* OFF TO BED WE HAD TO GO... RELUCTANTLY!

WE'LL NEVER FORGET THAT OLD KITCHEN!

WE HAD A SUSPICION THAT MAMA WANTED US OFF TO BED SO SHE COULD HELP PAPA! ANYWAY, SISTER SLEPT DOWNSTAIRS AND WE, UPSTAIRS. AFTER WE SAID OUR PRAYERS WE WENT TO THE WINDOW AND LOOKED OUT, UP AT THE STARLIT SKY. ONE STAR WAS MUCH BRIGHTER. IT SEEMED TO US TO BE THE STAR OF BETHLEHEM .....

YES, ...

PERHAPS IT WAS THAT GREAT, GALLANT LEADING STAR WE SAW IN THE SKY THAT NIGHT... OR MAYBE IT WAS JUST BECAUSE IT WAS *CHRISTMAS EVE!*

CHRISTMAS MORNING SPARKLED ..... BUT, WHAT HAPPENED ON THAT DAY IS STILL A MYSTERY. THERE WERE TOYS AND A THOUSAND MILLION JOYS, ENOUGH TO MAKE US FORGET.....
But,
WHEN THE TREE WAS LIGHTED IN THE OLD PARLOR, 'TWAS THEN THAT WE STARTED TO REMEMBER AGAIN ... AND WE CAPTURED A CHERISHED MEMORY...

ON THAT NIGHT AFTER THE NIGHT BEFORE CHRISTMAS!

AND SO, ONCE AGAIN WE HAVE TAKEN A JOURNEY INTO YESTERYEAR, "SURROUNDED" IN THE OLD CHILDHOOD NEIGHBORHOOD BY GOOD FOLKS ... JUST LIKE YOU AN' YOU AN' YOU! AS SOON AS WE REMEMBERED HOW OLD THE MEMORIES WERE, OUR STROLL ENDED! BUT, IN ANOTHER YEAR WE'LL BE ANXIOUS AGAIN TO SCAMPER DOWN CHRISTMAS MEMORY LANE!

The Miracle of the Birth of Christ

The Story of the Nativity

The oldest and most beautiful of all stories is the life of Mary, Joseph, and their son — Jesus.

For centuries and centuries, the Jews had waited for the Messiah promised to them by Jehovah. Patiently had they waited — and the promise and dream was fulfilled. Faith, which had grown dim during the years, was revived under the words of John, the forerunner.

As it is written in the prophets, Behold, I send my messenger before thy face, which shall prepare thy way before thee. The voice of one crying in the wilderness, Prepare ye the way of the Lord, make his paths straight.

Men and women bowed down in worship, repenting their sins while they awaited the Anointed One.

angel of the Lord came to Mary,
ing: *Hail, thou, that art highly
ured, the Lord is with thee : blessed art
u among women. Fear not, Mary:
hou hast found favour with God. And
ld, thou shall conceive in thy womb,
bring forth a son, and shalt call his
ne Jesus.*

while Joseph was alone in thought,
angel of heaven appeared to him
a dream, saying: *Joseph, thou son
David, fear not to take unto thee
y thy wife: for that which is conceived
er is of the Holy Ghost. And she
ll bring forth a son, and thou
ll call his name Jesus :
he shall save his people from their*

n Joseph, awakened from sleep,
as the angel bid, and went unto
wife.

At this time, Caesar Augustus ruler of the land, sent out a decree that all who lived there were to be taxed. Joseph and Mary were living in Nazareth, and the journey to Bethlehem was long and hard. Mary rode on a donkey while Joseph walked ahead, leading the donkey.

They were tired and weary when they reached Bethlehem, and the city was crowded. There was no room for them in the inns. The innkeepers saw that they were very poor, and did not want to bother with them. Finally, they knocked at the door of an inn at the edge of town. This innkeeper was a very kind man, and although he had no room in the inn, he said that they might sleep in the stable with the animals. Very thankful were Joseph and Mary for this shelter.

Inside the humble stable, Joseph gathered some of the fragrant hay and made a soft bed in one corner for Mary. She lay down and soon fell asleep in this strange place. The animals were curious to see who was sharing their home, and gathered about Mary and Joseph.

And she brought forth her first-born son, and wrapped him in swaddling clothes, and laid him in a manger; because there was no room for them in the inn.

A great light shone in the sky — and the shepherds in the field were afraid, for never before had they seen such a sight. An angel from the heavens above came to comfort them, saying:

Behold, I bring you good tidings
great joy, which shall be to all peop
For unto you is born this day in the
city of David a saviour, which is
Christ the Lord. And this shall be
sign unto you; Ye shall find the be
wrapped in swaddling clothes, lyi
in a manger.

And suddenly there was with the
angel a multitude of the heavenly
host praising God and saying, Glc
to God in the highest, and on earth
peace, good will toward men.

As the shepherds came to the sto
and found Mary and Joseph, a
the baby lying in the manger, th
fell on their knees and prayed t
the child who was their King. I
great exultation they returned t
their flock, telling other shepher
they met about the child, Jesus
their King, who was born in a mar

far off Persia, Three Wise Men
re looking in the sky and saw a
range star. As they watched, the
r told them of the baby, Jesus,
o was King of the world. The
se men hurriedly packed their
est gifts on their camels and
barked upon their journey to
thlehem to see the Christ Child.

took many days before they
rived in Bethlehem. They came,
ying: *Where is he that is born King*
he Jews? for we have seen his star in
east, and are come to worship him.

d when they were come into the house,
y saw the young child with Mary,
mother. They, too, fell on their
ees and prayed, presenting gifts
gold, frankincense, and myrrh
the child of Love.

Now, after the Wise Men left, an angel of the Lord appeared to Joseph in a dream, saying: Arise, and take the young child and his mother, and flee into Egypt, and be thou there until I bring thee word: for Herod will seek the young child to destroy him. When he arose, he took the young child and his mother, by night, and departed into Egypt.

There they lived until word came that Herod was dead. And he came and dwelt in a city called Nazareth: that it might be fulfilled which was spoken by the prophets, he shall be called a Nazarene.

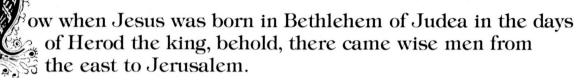

ow when Jesus was born in Bethlehem of Judea in the days of Herod the king, behold, there came wise men from the east to Jerusalem.

Saying, Where is he that is born King of the Jews? for we have seen his star in the east, and are come to worship him.

When Herod the king had heard these things, he was troubled, and all Jerusalem with him.

And when he had gathered all the chief priests and scribes of the people together, he demanded of them where Christ should be born.

And they said unto him, In Bethlehem of Judea: for thus it is written by the prophet,

And thou Bethlehem, in the land of Juda, art not the least among the princes of Juda: for out of thee shall come a Governor, that shall rule my people Israel.

Then Herod, when he had privily called the wise men, enquired of them diligently what time the star appeared.

And he sent them to Bethlehem, and said, Go and search diligently for the young child; and when ye have found him, bring me word again, that I may come and worship him also.

When they had heard the king, they departed; and, lo, the star, which they saw in the east, went before them, till it came and stood over where the young child was.

When they saw the star, they rejoiced with exceeding great joy.

And when they were come into the house, they saw the young child with Mary his mother, and fell down, and worshipped him: and when they had opened their treasures, they presented unto him gifts; gold, and frankincense, and myrrh.

And being warned of God in a dream that they should not return to Herod, they departed into their own country another way.

Matthew 2:1-12

The Man Who Brought The Myrrh

Shirley G. Robinson

The listening silence held its cold, sparkling arms about them, bringing Heaven close to the three tired travelers who, in spite of the excitement and wonder of the last few hours, had fallen asleep on the ground before the ebbing campfire.

Upon each countenance sleep carved a deep calmness, a serenity, a radiance which might be explained only by one who recognized the three as sages from the East who had just come from worship of the newly born King of the Jews.

Now they were on their way back to the king's palace to bring Herod news of the Child and of the place of his birth.

Beyond the hill a shimmering white light began to appear slowly, steadily. As it became brighter its radiance seemed to spread, illuminating the surrounding countryside. With a start, the travelers awakened and sat up as they heard a voice saying, "Behold."

Blinded by the brilliance and gasping with the glory of the man in the lustrous white robes, seemingly suspended on the path of light extending from the heavens, they uttered a cry of fear as of one man, and fell upon their faces.

107

Now in a gentle but penetrating voice, the angel spoke again. "Fear not, for behold! I come to you from the Father on High who has seen you this night in your worship of His Son, the Christ. I bring to you His message: Do not return to Herod with news of that which has just come to pass and which you have witnessed; for he is seeking the young Child — to Destroy him!"

As suddenly as it had appeared, the light began to tremble and fade and the angel rose into it and disappeared.

Now Herod waited many days for the return of the wise men. When he saw that he was being mocked by them he became exceedingly angry and sent forth his messengers to seek the Child themselves.

While they sought diligently for the Child, Herod rent his clothes and tore his hair in wrath and jealousy. He was now an old man, and knowing that his days upon the earth were numbered, he called together his chief priests. Suppose the throne should pass into the hands of this unknown "King of the Jews?" What would become of him in his last days and of his heirs?

By this time, Joseph, the father of Jesus, had been warned in a dream to take the Child and his mother and to flee into Egypt to remain until Herod's death.

Vainly seeking the Christ Child or word of Him, the messengers soon became weary and returned to the king only to be sent forth again into all parts of Bethlehem and the coasts thereof with the command to slay every child of two years and under, according to the time at which Herod had first inquired of the wise men where the King was to be born.

In this manner, surely the Child's destruction would be assured!

Before the return of the commissioners, however, Herod in his great wrath fell violently ill upon his bed and died, leaving the throne to his son.

And when Joseph had received this word from God, he took the Child Jesus and his mother into Galilee, making their dwelling in a place called Nazareth that it might be fulfilled which was spoken by the prophets, "He shall be called a Nazarene."

The threatening silence closed in about them, bringing Heaven close to the crowd thronging about the hillside. Out of the silence a sudden cry of unimaginable anguish escaped the lips of One hanging from a rough-hewn cross at the crest of a hill.

Upon his countenance even pain carved a deep calmness, a serenity, a radiance which could be explained most fully, perhaps, by an old man who slowly, haltingly, made his way through the mocking crowd to the foot of the hill where he laid his gift of

109

myrrh. Then he fell down, trembling, in worship of "his King."

The crowd moved back in silence as the heavens grew darker and darker, and a deeper peace settled over the face of the One hanging from the cross as he parted his lips for the final time····"Father, unto Thy hands, I commend my spirit".

The old man, tearfully, quietly, made his way back to the place where his camel waited.

Remembering that night years before, he thought of his two companions who had come with him to worship the Babe in the manger. What would they have thought—if they could have witnessed the scene which he had just witnessed?

Perhaps they had ····· and were even now preparing their gifts of heavenly gold and frankincense for the day when they would soon worship him again.

The Keeper Of The Inn
A Christmas Message
Bishop William P. Remington

There is an old story about the Keeper of the Inn, who owned the Stable where Jesus was born. The census was being taken by Caesar Augustus; roads were crowded with people going to their own cities and the Inn at Bethlehem was full to overflowing. For one thing Marcus Publius, a great man of Rome with his servants and his horses, his scribes and his guards, filled the place. The old Innkeeper was kept hurrying hither and yon and even then could not do all the things demanded of him. And all the time more travelers were coming and asking that they might abide there for the night.

There was One who came the next morning, whom the Innkeeper would not have turned away for all the silver in the world, if only he had known who He was. There were two of them, a man, who might have been a carpenter or a potter, and his wife sitting all doubled up upon a donkey.

The man said his wife was ill and could travel no farther. But the Innkeeper grew angry at his pleas, shouting at him, "Can I make more rooms arise by striking my staff upon the ground?"

And so the Innkeeper missed the greatest opportunity that ever an Innkeeper had. Long years afterwards it never did much good to repeat over and over again, "They were but poor folk and how was I to know?"

When afterwards the Child Jesus was born in the Stable and a great light filled all the heavens and there was a sound of heavenly music, Marcus Publius and his servants were still in a drunken sleep, and the Innkeeper had missed his great chance.

So it has been, and so it will be for many throughout the ages. Always there is that light in the heavens, that song in the air, that bright star, clear in the Eastern sky, which tell of the Birth of Christ. He comes to all and yet only a few see the light and run joyfully to the Manger Cradled King.

We each one are the Keepers of the Inn. Never were there so many people on the roads demanding an entrance to our hearts and homes. Even as we prepare for our Christmas, we have rushed hither and yon, like little ants storing food, or heaping up little hills of dust and dirt.

In countries like Russia, and her satellites, the roads have been crowded with wayfarers hurrying to be enrolled in Caesar's armies or to pay Caesar's taxes. Such "lords of creation" demand the whole Inn, every room, every service, every bit of food, and that is the reason why these countries have no use for Mary and her Child. Hate, envy and lust of empire fill the hearts of Dictators, as they did in the days of the Caesars, and of course we do not expect them to have any room left for the Christ Child.

But we Americans, we too are Keepers of the Inn. We have stores of food, and an abundance of room. We cannot say that our country is over-crowded or our resources overtaxed. We have more than they all, we Innkeepers at the World's Crossroads. If we could only open all our rooms, and share the gold we have in plenty, no one would go hungry this Christmas. What is it that makes us fail? Why do we repeat the same old excuse: "If I had only known?"

The tragedy of America is different from that of some countries in Europe and Asia. We have not been overcrowded, but we have been pre-occupied. There are not too many people in the Inn, but too much furniture. We have cluttered up the house with our possessions. Instead of the voices of Angels we have had to listen to high-pressure salesmen broadcast-ing their merchandise, their luxuries and their goods. Each day is marked off on a Calendar as a shopping Day until Christmas. And so days of preparation for the coming King are turned into hectic efforts to sell and buy, so that our Inn may be full: too full to hold Mary, Joseph and The Child.

The whole world is full of darkness this Christ-mas ... and yet, beyond the darkness of the earth's night the "Day spring from on High" can be seen by men of faith.

The Spirit of Giving

My Prayer . . .
. . . as a New Year Begins . . .

Mrs. J. Buick

O Lord, as on the threshold of another year I stand and turn the pages in my book of golden memories, I thank Thee, Lord, for all the lovely things therein I see, for all the sweet forget-me-nots of yesterday.

The scented woodland paths in memory once again I see where buttercups and primroses and violets smile at me; the lichen and the ivy clinging to the garden wall; and the perfume of the roses — I thank Thee, Lord, for all the wondrous things that life has given — for friends, both new and old, whose love has stood the test of years, whose hearts are hearts of gold.

For laughter, smiles and gladness, yes, and sympathizing tears; for those who shared the griefs and joys of all the bygone years; for shadows o'er the sunlit path; for pain that stayed awhile; for tender hands of loved ones who made glad that weary mile.

For graves upon the hillside where loved ones quietly sleep, where daffodils and crocuses in springtime softly peep. For the old church bell a-ringing that called us all to prayer; for the strains of organ music sweetly filling all the air; and the birds sang back an echo from the gently waving trees; their glad songs intermingled with the humming of the bees.

I thank Thee for a home where love is warm and strong and great; for loving smiles of welcome when they see me at the gate; for the sound of young folks laughter, for the coming of their feet; for their music in the twilight like a benediction sweet; for the prayers that rise at eventide when the work of day is done; and we gather round the altar at the setting of the sun.

I'd like to think that in the years that I may have in store, there will always be love's roses blooming all around my door; that the breeze will waft their petals to someone who is sad; that their beauty and their fragrance might a weary heart make glad. I'd like to think when I am through, that life had been worthwhile; that someone truly had been blest by my handclasp and my smile.

I do not ask to do great deeds nor have my name enscrolled, but just to keep on loving folks like Jesus did of old — content to do the little things that happiness may spring in hearts where hopes and dreams have died, where sorrow left its sting.

For there are many hearts that ache with weariness and pain, who feel perchance in retrospect, that life has been in vain; perhaps they're old with silvered hair, O help me, Lord, I pray, to cheer them on and help them keep their souls from turning grey.

So keep me always cheerful, Lord, that when I chance to meet my neighbor coming homeward along our quiet street, that I may never sadden her with any tale of care or add in any measure to the load she has to bear. But always let me think of something helpful I can say, that somehow she may feel so glad she met me by the way; perhaps from out the mists of doubt a stronger faith will rise and when we part she'll say 'goodbye' with laughter in her eyes.

Then when the tale of all my years at last is written down, it may be that my neighbor will be a jewel in my crown; but more than all, I want to hear in gentle tones from Thee, Thy gracious verdict, "Inasmuch — Ye did it unto Me."

And so, when in eternity, on the sea of glass I stand, and I see dear familiar faces round about on every hand, if someone might just come to me and clasp my hand and say, "I'm here because you smiled at me when I faltered by the way."

O with what joy I'll sing that song 'mid music rich and rare! Lord, grant me this I ask of Thee — this is my New Year Prayer.

©

A Christmas Meditation

Jeanne W. Rosenberger

I saw Christmas . . .

It was a beautiful thing to see.
It was all red and green, and sparkly in color.

It was tinselled stars, snow-clad hills, and
scented pine trees.
It was gay packages, colored lights, happy Santas,
and prancing reindeer.

It was stuffed turkey, cranberry sauce, pumpkin pie
and wished-for electric trains.
It was a stocking hung by the chimney, a sleepy
little boy, a warm crackling fire.

It was a humble bed of straw, a radiant mother,
a beautiful baby.

I heard Christmas . . .

As greetings were exchanged over the counter, and along the street.

I heard Christmas, from the choir as it was practicing a cantata, and from a group of carolers as they lifted their voices in the glorious harmony of "Silent Night."

I heard Christmas in the scuff of sandaled feet as shepherds and wise men crossed the fields to enter Bethlehem, bearing their treasured gifts.

I felt Christmas . . .

It was a beautiful thing to feel.
I felt it all around me, and it enfolded me
as a warm, soft cloak.
I felt it in the very cold tingle of the air.
I felt it in the mass of humanity moving around
me in a closer walk of brotherhood, where
quarrels are forgotten— wrongs righted— and
a smile on the face of all.

I felt Christmas in the very presence of
the newborn King.
I felt Him so near, I could almost touch the
hem of His garment.
I felt the true meaning and the spirit of Christmas,
as it renewed itself in each man's heart.
I felt that life and death again held purpose and
meaning through the birthday of a King!

I saw Christmas . . .
I heard Christmas . . .
I felt Christmas . . .

And I knew that, once again there would be
"Peace on earth, Good will toward all men."

THEY PRESENTED UNTO HIM GIFTS; GOLD, AND.... FRANKINCENSE, AND MYRRH.

MATTHEW 2:11

The Gift of the Magi

O. Henry

One dollar and eighty-seven cents. That was all. And sixty cents of it was in pennies. Pennies saved one and two at a time by bulldozing the grocer and the vegetable man and the butcher until one's cheeks burned with the silent imputation of parsimony that such close dealing implied. Three times Della counted it. One dollar and eighty-seven cents. And the next day would be Christmas.

There was clearly nothing to do but flop down on the shabby little couch and howl. So Della did it. Which instigates the moral reflection that life is made up of sobs, sniffles, and smiles, with sniffles predominating.

While the mistress of the home is gradually subsiding from the first stage to the second, take a look at the home. A furnished flat at $8 per week. It did not exactly beggar description, but it certainly had that word on the lookout for the mendicancy squad.

In the vestibule below was a letter-box into which no letter would go, and an electric button from which no mortal finger could coax a ring. Also appertaining thereunto was a card bearing the name "Mr. James Dillingham Young."

The "Dillingham" had been flung to the breeze during a former period of prosperity when its possessor was being paid $30 per week. Now, when the income was shrunk to $20, letters of "Dillingham" looked blurred, as though they were thinking seriously of contracting to a modest and unassuming D. But whenever Mr. James Dillingham Young came home and reached his flat above he was called "Jim" and greatly hugged by Mrs. James Dillingham Young, already introduced to you as Della. Which is all very good.

Della finished her cry and attended to her cheeks with the powder rag. She stood by the window and looked out dully at a grey cat walking a grey fence in a grey backyard. Tomorrow would be Christmas Day, and she had only $1.87 with which to buy Jim a present. She had been saving every penny she could for months, with this result. Twenty dollars a week doesn't go far. Expenses had been greater than she had calculated. They always are. Only $1.87 to buy a present for Jim. Her Jim. Many a happy hour she had spent planning for something nice for him. Something fine and rare and sterling—something just a little bit near to being worthy of the honour of being owned by Jim.

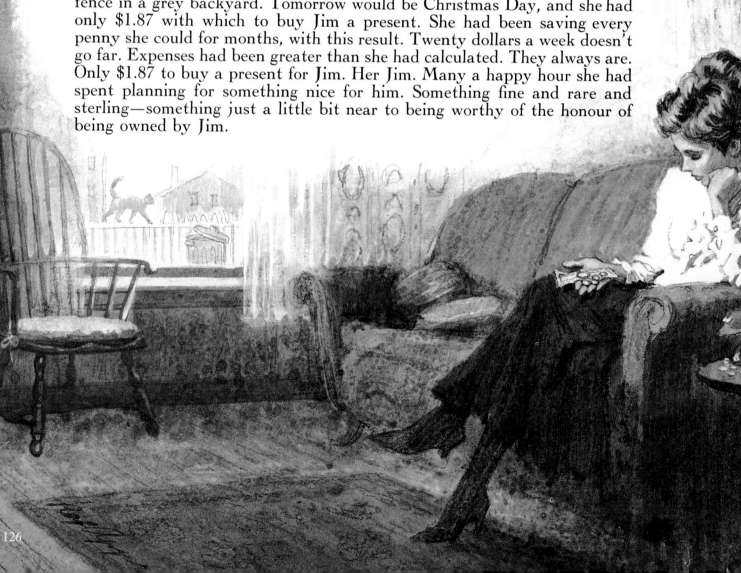

There was a pier-glass between the windows of the room. Perhaps you have seen a pier-glass in an $8 flat. A very thin and very agile person may, by observing his reflection in a rapid sequence of longitudinal strips, obtain a fairly accurate conception of his looks. Della, being slender had mastered the art.

Suddenly she whirled from the window and stood before the glass. Her eyes were shining brilliantly, but her face had lost its colour within twenty seconds. Rapidly she pulled down her hair and let it fall to its full length.

Now, there were two possessions of the James Dillingham Youngs in which they both took a mighty pride. One was Jim's gold watch that had been his father's and his grandfather's. The other was Della's hair. Had the Queen of Sheba lived in the flat across the airshaft, Della would have let her hair hang out the window some day to dry just to depreciate Her Majesty's jewels and gifts. Had King Solomon been the janitor, with all his treasures piled up in the basement, Jim would have pulled out his watch every time he passed, just to see him pluck at his beard from envy.

So now Della's beautiful hair fell about her, rippling and shining like a cascade of brown waters. It reached below her knee and made itself almost a garment for her. And then she did it up again nervously and quickly. Once she faltered for a minute and stood still while a tear or two splashed on the worn red carpet.

On went her old brown jacket; on went her old brown hat. With a whirl of skirts and with the brilliant sparkle still in her eyes, she fluttered out the door and down the stairs to the street.

Where she stopped the sign read: "Mme. Sofronie. Hair Goods of All Kinds." One flight up Della ran, and collected herself, panting. Madame, large, too white, chilly, hardly looked the "Sofronie."

"Will you buy my hair?" asked Della.

"I buy hair," said Madame. "Take yer hat off and let's have a sight at the looks of it."

Down rippled the brown cascade.

"Twenty dollars," said Madame, lifting the mass with a practised hand.

"Give it to me quick," said Della.

Oh, and the next two hours tripped by on rosy wings. Forget the hashed metaphor. She was ransacking the stores for Jim's present.

She found it at last. It surely had been made for Jim and no one else. There was no other like it in any of the stores, and she had turned all of them inside out. It was a platinum fob chain simple and chaste in design, properly proclaiming its value by substance alone and not by meretricious ornamentation—as all good things do. It was even worthy of The Watch. As soon as she saw it she knew that it must be Jim's. It was like him. Quietness and value—the description applied to both. Twenty-one dollars they took from her for it, and she hurried home with 87 cents. With that chain on his watch Jim might be properly anxious about the time in any company. Grand as the watch was, he sometimes looked at it on the sly on account of the old leather strap that he used in place of a chain.

When Della reached home her intoxication gave way a little to prudence and reason. She got out her curling irons and lighted the gas and went to work repairing the ravages made by generosity added to love. Which is always a tremendous task, dear friends—a mammoth task.

Within forty minutes her head was covered by tiny, close-lying curls that made her look wonderfully like a truant schoolboy. She looked at her reflection in the mirror long, carefully, and critically.

"If Jim doesn't kill me," she said to herself, "before he takes a second look at me, he'll say I look like a Coney Island chorus girl. But what could I do—oh! what could I do with a dollar and eighty-seven cents?"

At 7 o'clock the coffee was made and the frying-pan was on the back of the stove hot and ready to cook the chops.

Jim was never late. Della doubled the fob chain in her hand and sat on the corner of the table near the door that he always entered. Then she heard his step on the stair away down on the first flight, and she turned white for just a moment. She had a habit of saying little silent prayers about the simplest everyday things, and now she whispered: "Please God, make him think I am still pretty."

The door opened and Jim stepped in and closed it. He looked thin and very serious. Poor fellow, he was only twenty-two—and to be burdened with a family! He needed a new overcoat and he was without gloves.

Jim stopped inside the door, as immovable as a setter at the scent of quail. His eyes were fixed upon Della, and there was an expression in them that she could not read, and it terrified her. It was not anger, nor surprise, nor disapproval, nor horror, nor any of the sentiments that she had been prepared for. He simply stared at her fixedly with that peculiar expression on his face.

Della wriggled off the table and went for him.

"Jim, darling," she cried, "don't look at me that way. I had my hair cut off and sold it because I couldn't have lived through Christmas without giving you a present. It'll grow out again—you won't mind, will you? I just had to do it. My hair grows awfully fast. Say 'Merry Christmas!' Jim, and let's be happy. You don't know what a nice—what a beautiful, nice gift I've got for you."

"You've cut off your hair?" asked Jim, laboriously, as if he had not arrived at that patent fact yet even after the hardest mental labour.

"Cut it off and sold it," said Della. "Don't you like me just as well, anyhow? I'm me without my hair, ain't I?"

"You say your hair is gone?" he said, with an air almost of idiocy.

"You needn't look for it," said Della. "It's sold, I tell you—sold and gone, too. It's Christmas Eve, boy. Be good to me, for it went for you. Maybe the hairs of my head were numbered," she went on with a sudden serious sweetness, "but nobody could ever count my love for you. Shall I put the chops on, Jim?"

Out of his trance Jim seemed quickly to wake. He enfolded his Della. For ten seconds let us regard with discreet scrutiny some inconsequential object in the other direction. Eight dollars a week or a million a year—what is the difference? A mathematician or a wit would give you the wrong answer. The magi brought valuable gifts, but that was not among them. This dark assertion will be illuminated later on.

Jim drew a package from his overcoat pocket and threw it upon the table.

"Don't make any mistake, Dell," he said, "about me. I don't think there's anything in the way of a haircut or a shave or a shampoo that could make me like my girl any less. But if you'll unwrap that package you may see why you had me going a while at first."

White fingers and nimble tore at the string and paper. And then an ecstatic scream of joy; and then, alas! a quick feminine change to hysterical tears and wails, necessitating the immediate employment of all the comforting powers of the lord of the flat.

For there lay The Combs—the set of combs, side and back, that Della had worshipped for long in a Broadway window. Beautiful combs, pure tortoise shell, with jeweled rims—just the shade to wear in the beautiful vanished hair. They were expensive combs, she knew, and her heart had simply craved and yearned over them without the least hope of possession. And now, they were hers, but the tresses that should have adorned the coveted adornments were gone.

But she hugged them to her bosom, and at length she was able to look up with dim eyes and a smile and say: "My hair grows so fast, Jim!"

And then Della leaped up like a little singed cat and cried, "Oh, oh!"

Jim had not yet seen his beautiful present. She held it out to him eagerly upon her open palm. The dull precious metal seemed to flash with a reflection of her bright and ardent spirit.

"Isn't it a dandy, Jim? I hunted all over town to find it. You'll have to look at the time a hundred times a day now. Give me your watch. I want to see how it looks on it."

Instead of obeying, Jim tumbled down on the couch and put his hands under the back of his head and smiled.

"Dell," said he, "let's put our Christmas presents away and keep 'em a while. They're too nice to use just at present. I sold the watch to get the money to buy your combs. And now suppose you put the chops on."

The magi, as you know, were wise men—wonderfully wise men—who brought gifts to the Babe in the manger. They invented the art of giving Christmas presents. Being wise, their gifts were no doubt wise ones, possibly bearing the privilege of exchange in case of duplication. And here I have lamely related to you the uneventful chronicle of two foolish children in a flat who most unwisely sacrificed for each other the greatest treasures of their house. But in a last word to the wise of these days let it be said that of all who give gifts these two were the wisest. Of all who give and receive gifts, such as they are wisest. Everywhere they are wisest. They are the magi.

Celebration of Song

STORY OF THE CHRISTMAS BELLS

Long, long ago, in a tiny village called Lusanne, there was a beautiful little church which all the people loved. This church had been built by their forefathers, generations ago, from the stones and logs on their farms. It stood on a high hill, watching over the peasant homes in the valley.

From outside appearances, the church was no different than many others, but inside it was the most beautiful of all, for it reflected the love and spirit of its people. In one corner stood an old brown organ which accompanied the people as they sang their hymns, and in the center of the church stood a hand-carved pulpit which had been made by the best carpenter of the village.

The people of this tiny village had always dreamed of having beautiful silver bells in their church steeple, but they were very poor and could not afford them. Year after year they hoped to save enough money to buy these bells which would make their church complete, but the church steeple had remained empty.

Nevertheless, the people loved their church and each year, on Christmas Eve, people came from near and far to enjoy the beautiful Christmas program. And, because it was Christmas, those who would attend brought their most precious gift to lay at the foot of the altar in honor of the Child of Love.

Far, far away from Lusanne, there lived two little girls, Mary and Margaret, who were daughters of a very poor and humble peasant farmer. The little girls were too young to understand why they could not afford to travel to the church in Lusanne, but they had heard about the beautiful service and wanted to be in the church on Christmas Eve. And at night, when they were alone, they would talk about going to Lusanne, and then they decided on a secret plan.

"Nobody knows," Mary said, *"how many wonderful gifts are laid at the altar, and the people can never tell others of the beauty and love in the church on Christmas Eve. You have to be there to see it. An old man who was traveling through the country, on his way to teach school at Lusanne, told us that the church was very old and that it was the most beautiful in all the land."*

The afternoon before Christmas was bitterly cold, and snowflakes were quickly covering the earth. Unknown to their family, Mary and Margaret quietly tip-toed out of the house and started on their long journey to the pretty church. Bundled in their heaviest coats and boots, the little girls trudged through the snow. Before sundown they had traveled many miles and were nearing the first farmhouse on the edge of the village. As they came nearer to the farmhouse, they saw that it was barren and deserted. Tired and weary from the long journey, they decided to go into the empty house to rest for a few minutes before going further. The door was ajar, and they walked in. There were no chairs, so the little girls sat on the floor.

And as they talked, they heard a strange, low sounding noise. They stopped to listen—but all was again silent. A few minutes later they heard the same sound. Mary quickly jumped up and ran into the next room. And there, lying in a corner, was a baby lamb. As the little girls knelt to stroke it, the lamb tried to move—*the little girls leaned closer and then they saw that the little white lamb had broken its leg.*

A mile or more before they came to the farmhouse, they had seen tracks in the snow and wondered where they had come from, for no one was in sight. The little lamb must have strayed from the flock and broken its leg while trying to climb the hills. It had come to this house for shelter from the snow and cold.

Mary and Margaret knelt down to see if they could carry the lamb to Lusanne, to get help, but as the girls touched the lamb, its mournful bleat filled their hearts with sympathy.

"No, we cannot move the lamb, little sister, so you will have to go to Lusanne alone." "All alone?" cried Margaret, "and you won't see the pretty church?" "No," sobbed Mary, "for we can't leave this tiny lamb alone. It is frightened by the cold and the pain in its leg. Everyone has left for church now, but when you come back after the service, bring some-one to help me. Maybe a farmer could fix the lamb's leg here and we wouldn't have to move it. You go on to the church, Margaret, and I'll stay with the little lamb and stroke it so it won't feel alone. And, after a while, I'll feed it some snow and the cookie that is left in my pocket."

"But I can't go alone," sobbed Margaret, "Yes, you must," said Mary. "You know your way to the church, and the little lamb needs help. It is in great pain. When you are in the church you must watch carefully every minute so you can tell me every-thing. I'm sure Jesus knows how much I want to be in the church, and He will understand. If you can get near the altar without bothering anyone, little sister, take this locket of mine and, when no one is looking, put it at the foot of the altar as my offering."

Reluctantly Margaret left, and Mary tried hard to keep the tears from falling. All year long they had planned this night when they would see the beauti-

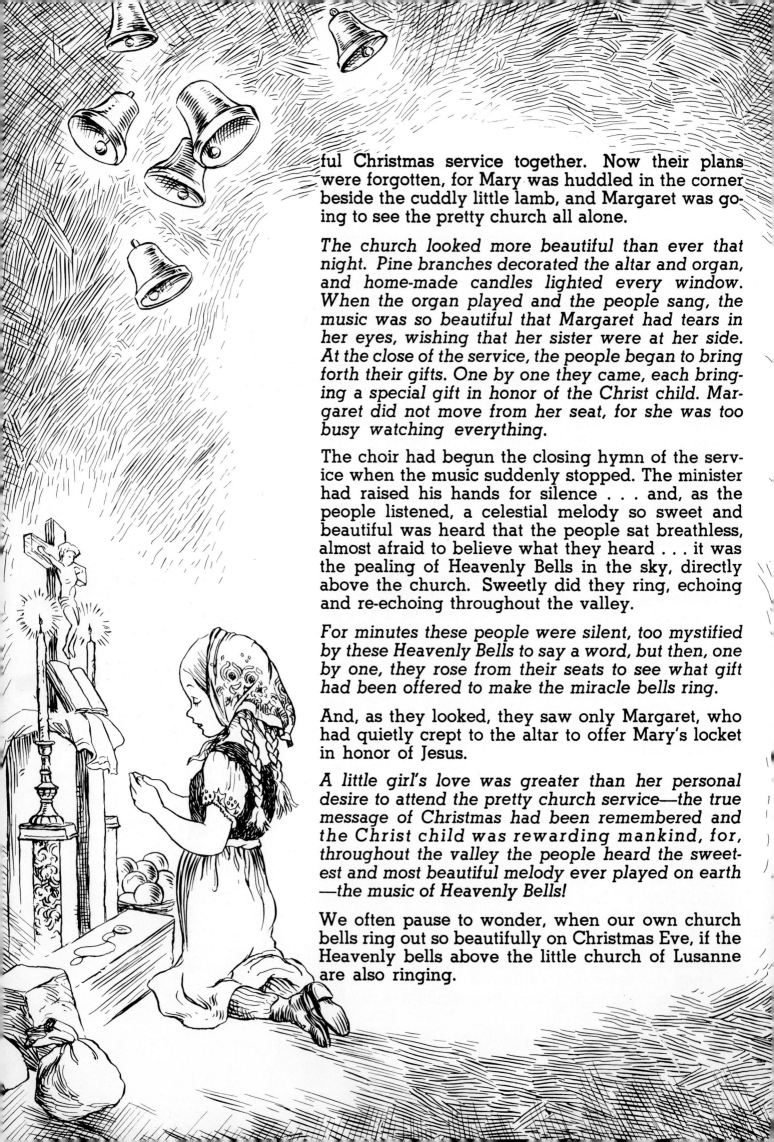

ful Christmas service together. Now their plans were forgotten, for Mary was huddled in the corner beside the cuddly little lamb, and Margaret was going to see the pretty church all alone.

The church looked more beautiful than ever that night. Pine branches decorated the altar and organ, and home-made candles lighted every window. When the organ played and the people sang, the music was so beautiful that Margaret had tears in her eyes, wishing that her sister were at her side. At the close of the service, the people began to bring forth their gifts. One by one they came, each bringing a special gift in honor of the Christ child. Margaret did not move from her seat, for she was too busy watching everything.

The choir had begun the closing hymn of the service when the music suddenly stopped. The minister had raised his hands for silence . . . and, as the people listened, a celestial melody so sweet and beautiful was heard that the people sat breathless, almost afraid to believe what they heard . . . it was the pealing of Heavenly Bells in the sky, directly above the church. Sweetly did they ring, echoing and re-echoing throughout the valley.

For minutes these people were silent, too mystified by these Heavenly Bells to say a word, but then, one by one, they rose from their seats to see what gift had been offered to make the miracle bells ring.

And, as they looked, they saw only Margaret, who had quietly crept to the altar to offer Mary's locket in honor of Jesus.

A little girl's love was greater than her personal desire to attend the pretty church service—the true message of Christmas had been remembered and the Christ child was rewarding mankind, for, throughout the valley the people heard the sweetest and most beautiful melody ever played on earth—the music of Heavenly Bells!

We often pause to wonder, when our own church bells ring out so beautifully on Christmas Eve, if the Heavenly bells above the little church of Lusanne are also ringing.

Silent Night

Joseph Mohr.   Franz Grüber.

1. Si - lent night, ho - ly night, All is calm, all is bright;
2. Si - lent night, ho - ly night, Dark-ness flies, all is light;
3. Si - lent night, ho - ly night, Won-drous Star, lend thy light;

Round yon Vir - gin Moth-er and Child! Ho-ly In-fant, so ten-der and mild,
Shep-herds hear the an — gels sing, "Al-le lu - ia! hail the King!
With the an-gels let us sing, Al-le lu - ia to our King;

Sleep in heaven-ly peace,   Sleep in heaven-ly peace.
Christ the Saviour is born, Christ the Saviour is born."
Christ the Saviour is born, Christ the Saviour is born. A - men.

O Come, All Ye Faithful

John Reading

1. O come, all ye faith-ful, joy-ful and tri-umphant, O come ye, O
2. Sing, choirs of an-gels, sing in ex-ul-ta-tion, O sing, all ye
3. Yea, Lord, we greet Thee, born this happy morning, Je-sus, to

come ye to Beth-le-hem! Come and be-hold Him, born the King of an-gels!
cit-i-zens of heav'n a-bove! Glo-ry to God, all glo-ry in the high-est!
Thee be all glo-ry giv'n; Word of the Fa-ther, now in flesh ap-pear-ing!

O come, let us a-dore Him, O come, let us a-dore Him, O come, let us a-

dore Him, Christ, the Lord! A — men.

Adeste Fideles

moderato marziale

come all ye faithful, joy-ful and tri-

um-ph, come ye to

Beth-

hold Him, born the King of Angels!

Oh, Night Divine

Marion H. Repp

'Tis night! And all the world now sinks
In slumber and in sweet forgetfulness;
A holy calm pervades the atmosphere,
And all is still!

All? No, for far away across the hills there come
The strains of distant music;
'Adeste Fideles' falls upon our eager waiting ears;
Yes! It is the glad commemoration
Of Christ our Savior's birth.

Oh, night divine! Backward we turn historic pages
Almost two thousand years;
We, upon the wings of our imagination,
Are wafted far away from this, our homeland,
Only to find ourselves among the old Judean hills,
Silent in the moonlight,
While before us pass in review those events
That mark this happy night, this night divine.

Oh, peaceful night! The world within God's keeping
Lies serene and still;
On the hillsides, guarded by the faithful shepherds,
The flocks are in repose

While nestled close upon one young lad's bosom
Sleeps his small white lamb, the pet of all the flock,
Safe from all harm.
All nature seems to give a contribution
To make this night a night of peace and quiet.

Oh, stilly night! And yet a night succeeding
A day of much commotion in the quiet streets
Of little Bethlehem;
For were not her streets and dwellings filled all day
With those who came to be enrolled
In this, their native city?
Were not at this, the evening hour, her inns all filled?

And yet, behold, yon pilgrims who have
But lately reached the town;
Weary, indeed, is he who leads the donkey
On which rides his companion,
Whose sweet and wistful face expresses thankfulness
That here, at last, may rest and lodging be found.
But can it here be found? Ah, no!
The inns are filled;
In vain does Joseph seek admittance, only to be told,
"There is no room!"
Till sadly back to Mary he returns and says,
"Our only shelter is yon lowly stable; let us go thence."
The cattle share with them their dwelling; silence reigns
On this, the stilly night.

Oh, glorious night! Hark, what songs angelic choirs are singing!
Hear what melodious sweetness falls upon the midnight air!
What means the message "Gloria in excelsis," the wondering shepherds ask,
As roused from slumber they observe celestial brightness;
Leaving their flocks, across the hills they hurry;
They seek their King; a star points out His dwelling,
A star of such uncommon brightness
Which leads them to the lowly stable
Where lies the King!
In humble adoration they kneel before Him,
His bed a manger bare
On this, the glorious night.

Oh, holy night! Not only shepherds
Did see the guiding star;
Behold, at the stable door appear three of lordly mien
Who also would do homage to the King.
Days had they spent, the while their trusty camels,
Careening over hills and plains and deserts,
Had safely brought them to their journey's end;
Sages from the farthest corners of the earth are they,
Their guide, the kindly star.

Gifts bring they, the choicest of their lands,
Which they present their King;
The little shepherd lad holds tightly in his arms his one pet lamb,
'Tis all he has.
Only for an instant does he hold it; and, then,
He places it beside the gold and perfumes rare,
The tributes of Balthasar, Gaspar and Melchior
Who now depart.
The Baby smiles, the Mother speaks unto the shepherd lad and says,
"Thy King is pleased with thee."
The guests depart; Mary croons a lullaby;
Oh, holiest of nights!

Oh, night of great rejoicing! The vision fades;
No longer stand we on Judea's hills;
Again we hear the music softly stealing
Upon the midnight air;
"Venite, adoremus," sing they, the echoes swelling round the earth
While peal the bells, "Peace on earth, good will to men,"
As down the ages it has come, the celebration
Of that great night.

Joy To The World!

Isaac Watts

George F. Händel

1. Joy to the world! the Lord is come: Let earth re-
2. Joy to the world! the Sav - iour reigns: Let men their
3. No more let sins and sor - rows grow, Nor thorns in-

ceive her King; Let ev - ery heart pre-pare Him room,
songs em - ploy; While fields and floods, rocks hills and plains,
fest the ground; He comes to make His bless - ings flow

And heaven and na-ture sing, And heaven and na-ture
Re - peat the sounding joy, Re - peat the sounding
Far as the curse is found, Far as the curse is

sing, And heaven, and heaven and na - ture sing.
joy, Re - peat, re - peat the sound-ing joy.
found, Far as, far as the curse is found.

Christmas in Many Lands

Christmas In Many Lands

Sweden

St. Lucia, dressed in white with a brilliant red sash about her waist and wearing an astonishing crown of pine boughs haloed with the light of seven candles, awakens the members of the household by bringing them coffee and cakes on a tray, thereby proclaiming the arrival of the Christmas season on December 13th.

A belief of Sweden is that ancestors come back to their former homes on Christmas Eve; and so, according to tradition, the living behave as intruders for the night as they make up the beds and prepare the tables for their ancestors.

Swedish holiday celebrations end on Christmas Eve with tree-trimming, dancing, singing, a dinner of "lutfisk," and the opening of the Christmas presents which are sealed with red wax.

Greece

December 25th is a happy day for the people of Greece, for it is the time of family reunions, parties, and merry-making. Remembering a custom of long ago, Greek mothers again make their famous fried cakes, while the little children watch in wide-eyed wonder, listening to the stories and old folk legends.

One of the most colorful legends is that of the Karkantzari — mysterious half-human and half-monster beings who wander about on the twelve days after Christmas and attempt to make mischief. The peasants call upon the priest to make the Karkantzari disappear until next year. A cross, entwined with sprigs of basil, is dipped into a copper vessel of Holy Water, and then each room of the farm house is sprinkled.

To further assure that these mysterious beings will not appear, old leather shoes, saved throughout the year, are burned, and the odor is believed to chase away these mischief-makers.

Sicily

Mountain musicians, playing melancholy melodies upon a violin and cello as they stroll through the village streets, set the picturesque Christmas scene in Sicily.

A pyramid-shaped altar, adorned with a waxen image of the Christ Child, is built in each home and church. Every evening, for nine days before Christmas, the altar is lighted and the people proclaim their devotion. Carols are sung in the homes, while in the church, strolling musicians perform scenes from the story of Christ's birth in the lowly manger.

A midnight mass is held on Christmas Eve. Following the religious service and carol singing, the people form a procession which is led by the priest, carrying the waxen image of the Christ Child. As the procession slowly winds through the town, fires are lighted in the squares — church bells are rung — and rockets are sent up to the sky.

After the "birth of the bambino" has been acclaimed by all, good wishes are exchanged and all return to their homes to enjoy the delicacies of the Christmas dinner.

Philippine Islands

Colorful wreaths and chains, made of brilliant tropical flowers, are worn by the Filipino children as they partake in the festive after-mass parade. A band leads the parade, providing the music for the children's singing.

In keeping with the significant religious spirit of the Christmas season, a family dinner follows the after-mass parade. Dancing and musical entertainment provide the remaining celebrations for the afternoon and evening.

The Filipino children do not have a Christmas tree — but they decorate their homes with lavish care. Flags, bunting, palms, and the many colorful flowers adorn their homes, and a candle is kept burning in the window all night long.

Concluding the celebrations of Christmas day, melodious church bells are heard ringing throughout the land until the last stroke of the clock proclaims that Christmas day has ended.

Bulgaria

With the appearance of the first star on Christmas Eve, the strict two weeks' fast is broken. A large round cake, called *kravai*, is decorated with the figures of a bird, a flower, and a cross, and is lighted by a candle. Incense is burned and prayers are offered before the husband and wife break a "good luck" piece from the ceremonial cake.

Christmas Day is begun with a church service, after which the children receive their gifts from Grandpa Koleda — the Bulgarian Santa Claus. As in days of old, the children present their parents with a remembrance on the eve of the last day of the old year.

Before breakfast on Christmas Day, the father of the family brings in the yule log, while the other members of the family sprinkle him with corn — a custom which is followed to bring health to all and a plenteous crop the following year. Kernels of corn are placed in a stocking, and some is also sprinkled upon the doorstep for additional assurance that the new year will be joyous. As the father lights the yule log, the children strike it, proclaiming their wishes as the sparks fly into the air.

Christmas In Many Lands

Denmark

"Jul-Nisse," the benevolent little man of the attic, is the essence of Christmas for many people in Denmark. Although he is seen by no one except the family cat, this little man, who lives in the attic and tends the farm animals, is responsible for many mischievous happenings in the house.

Before going to bed on Christmas Eve, the Danish children climb the attic stairs and place a bowl of porridge and a pitcher of milk before the door. They arise early the next morning, only to find that the food has mysteriously disappeared during the night.

One of Denmark's prettiest customs is the remembrance of the birds. A sheaf of grain is saved from the fall harvest—and on Christmas morning, every gable, gateway and barndoor is decorated with this bundle of grain—the birds' Christmas dinner.

155

Christmas In Many Lands

Poland

One of the most beautiful celebrations of the religious traditions of Christmas is offered to the world by Poland.

When the first star appears in the evening sky on December 24, Fast Day is ended and the Christmas supper begins. Straw is placed under the table, dishes, and tablecloth, and one chair is left vacant for the Holy Child. Symbolizing peace on earth is the Peace Wafer, procured from the priest and given to the head of the family to break and share with the guests. While the sacred wafer is being eaten, wishes for the coming year are exchanged.

Puppet shows, called "schopka," depicting the murder of the innocents by Herod, are given during the holidays. It is said that on Christmas night the heavens open and those who have lived pure and blameless lives can see the vision of Jacob's ladder.

The Polish Christmas centers around the songs which are a combination of the religious and secular sentiments of the people, sung in memory of the Savior's birth.

Christmas In Many Lands

Italy

Eclipsing the Christmas festival in Italy is the Feast of the Immaculate Conception, honoring the Virgin Mary. Calabrian shepherds, dressed in goat-skin trousers and colorful jackets, come down from the mountains to play on their pipes and pastoral flutes, stopping before each shrine in the streets and before the doors of all carpenter shops to salute the Virgin and Child.

Italy's Christmas scene is set with a profusion of pretty flowers and graceful olive trees. Their Santa Claus is the beneficent old witch, "Befano" who, clothed in rags, rides from house to house on a broomstick, leaving presents beside the hearth for the children.

The Precipio, truly symbolic of the Italian Christmas, is found in every home with tiny statuettes of the Holy Family, angels, shepherds and Wise Men grouped about a miniature manger.

Christmas In Many Lands

England

*On Christmas Eve the Yule log is brought ins
and placed in the big fireplace. According
custom, each person in the family must sit up
the log and salute it before it is lighted to ass
good luck for the household in the new yea*

Religious services predominate in the Engl
Christmas celebrations. Processions of caro
gather under the lofty arches of great cathed
at midnight on Christmas Eve to sing the old a
cherished hymns and carols. Christmas mu
mers are today enacting the same traditio
plays which have been presented for the p
several hundred years. Many of these pla
purely regional in character, bespeak Norma
Saxon, Viking and ancient British origins.

Christmas In Many Lands

Switzerland

"Samichlaus," as he is known in Switzerland, is eagerly awaited by the children on December 5th. In the mountain hamlets he is heralded with a procession from the little village church. Cross bearer and banner boys, wearing quaint, high-peaked hoods for protection from the mountain air and snow, lead the choir and clergy through the street. In their midst is the Saint himself—Samichlaus—wearing a red, jovial mask, white flowing beard, fur-trimmed robe, and a gray sack and staff, both conveying rewards for the good and bad children.

Samichlaus is met in the streets of the larger cities by happy, applauding children. He is usually a young bishop, accompanied by grotesquely masked attendant bishops carrying the triple purse associated with St. Nicholas. While the good bishop distributes apples and cookies, the attendant bishops collect alms.

159

Christmas Spirit
E. C. Baird

I am the Christmas Spirit!

I enter the home of poverty, causing palefaced children to open their eyes wide, in pleased wonder.

I cause the miser's clutched hand to relax, and thus paint a bright spot on his soul.

I cause the aged to renew their youth and to laugh in the old, glad way.

I keep romance alive in the heart of childhood, and brighten sleep with dreams woven of magic.

I cause eager feet to climb dark stairways with filled baskets, leaving behind hearts amazed at the goodness of the world.

I cause the prodigal to pause a moment on his wild, wasteful way, and send to anxious love some little token that releases glad tears — tears which wash away the hard lines of sorrow.

I enter dark prison cells, reminding scarred manhood of what might have been, and pointing forward to good days yet to be.

I come softly into the still, white home of pain, and lips that are too weak to speak just tremble in silent, eloquent gratitude.

In a thousand ways I cause the weary world to look up into the face of God, and for a little moment forget the things that are small and wretched.

I am the Christmas spirit!